SEX EDUCATION AND COUNSELING OF SPECIAL GROUPS

SEX EDUCATION AND COUNSELING OF SPECIAL GROUPS

THE MENTALLY AND PHYSICALLY HANDICAPPED, ILL AND ELDERLY

By

WARREN R. JOHNSON, Ed.D.

Professor of Health Education
Director, Children's Health and Developmental Clinic
University of Maryland
College Park, Maryland

220605

CHARLES C THOMAS · PUBLISHER
Springfield · Illinois · U.S.A.

Published and Distributed Throughout the World by
CHARLES C THOMAS • PUBLISHER
Bannerstone House
301-327 East Lawrence Avenue, Springfield, Illinois, U.S.A.

© 1975, by CHARLES C THOMAS • PUBLISHER
ISBN 0-398-03197-5
Library of Congress Catalog Card Number 74-7323

With THOMAS BOOKS *careful attention is given to all details of
manufacturing and design. It is the Publisher's desire to present books
that are satisfactory as to their physical qualities and artistic possibilities
and appropriate for their particular use.* THOMAS BOOKS *will be true
to those laws of quality that assure a good name and good will.*

Printed in the United States of America
W-2

Library of Congress Cataloging in Publication Data

Johnson, Warren Russell, 1921-
    Sex education and counseling of special groups.

    1. Sex instruction. 2. Counseling. I. Title.
[DNLM: 1. Counseling. 2. Sex education. 3. Handicapped.
HQ35.2 J71s 1974]
HQ56.J59   612.6'007   74-7323
ISBN 0-398-03197-5

Dedication

for Julie
with love and gratitude

CONTENTS

SEX EDUCATION AND COUNSELING
OF SPECIAL GROUPS

PART I

INTRODUCTION

Sᴇᴠᴇɴᴛᴇᴇɴ ʏᴇᴀʀs ᴀɢᴏ, I began conducting what we now call the Children's Health and Developmental Clinic for children with various physical and mental disorders at the University of Maryland. An education and counseling program was initiated for parents to attend during the children's program, and it soon became apparent that one of the parents' prominent needs was for education and counseling concerning the sexuality of their children. Sex education was therefore provided as one of the several child health and development topics considered in the eight-week series. Sex counseling was a natural outgrowth of the educational undertaking, with parents bringing up problems associated with their children either in the classroom setting or seeking a private conversation as they chose.

Some years earlier I had initiated a sex education program for teachers, undergraduate and graduate students at the University. The paucity of adequate literature on the subject led to publication of *Human Sexual Behavior and Sex Education: with Historical, Moral, Legal, Linguistic and Cultural Perspectives,*[1] and various articles to meet what seemed to be rather glaring needs. These writings were instrumental in bringing me into close contact with the relatively few leaders in the field who were attempting, through writing, research, teaching and organizations, to foster improved public understanding of sexuality. As a result, it was relatively easy to provide clinic parents with current basic information about common sexual

---

[1] W. R. Johnson and E. G. Belzer, Jr., *Human Sexual Behavior and Sex Education: with Historical, Moral, Legal, Linguistic and Cultural Perspectives,* 3rd ed. (Philadelphia, Lea & Febiger, 1973).

3

interests, behaviors and problems of children and youth. However, application of basic knowledge to clinic children was sometimes even more difficult than application to children in general.

In the first place, the clinic children are different in some way or ways. It is axiomatic in the child development field that children grow in their own way and at their own rate, and that growth and development are likely to be uneven. Children do not progress physically, emotionally, socially or intellectually at a uniform rate. They may be unusually big but poorly coordinated, unusually small but very bright and emotionally mature, or bright but socially inept, and so on. The clinic kids often carry uniqueness and unevenness to extremes. Consequently, it was necessary to be alert to the fact that the child's "specialness" might well entail unusual demands upon parents with regard to sex education.

In the second place, the clinic children are often perceived by virtually everyone as being different in general rather than specific ways. For example, what might easily pass for normal developmental events or individual differences in other children tends to be viewed as part of the problem of the special child, whether it is mental retardation, "minimal brain injury," cerebral palsy, hyperactivity, a psychiatric disorder or some degree of physical disability including even a malfunctioning limb or deafness. Obviously, sexual interests and behaviors in clinic children are especially likely to attract attention, to be associated with their disability, and, therefore, considered abnormal. Actually, behaviors that might well be considered healthy signs of masculinity or femininity in other children are often perceived as symptomatic in these special children, as in special children and adults elsewhere.

Here again, I found little in existing literature to pass on to the children's parents or their teachers. As I made worthwhile connections between current sex knowledge and the needs of parents and teachers in their dealings with the sexuality of their "special" children, I published some articles intended to be helpful to these and other groups. Sexuality of the mentally retarded seemed to be of special concern at the time, so my articles were focused on that group. However, much of the content applied to other groups such as the nonretarded in the clinic.

The absurdity of this situation gradually began to dawn upon me. Two major and related interests of mine, child health and development and sex education, chanced to converge in a hobby, the clinic—and after a little writing, I was suddenly an authority on the sex education of the mentally retarded and other special groups. There was no keeping up with requests for presentations on the subject, locally or in distant cities. "Why," I would sometimes ask gatherings, "is it necessary for you to import a speaker from hundreds of miles away when your own people have been dealing with the sexuality of special groups for years?"

Of course, the answer to this question summarizes what may be the basic problem in this field: one socially unacceptable phenomenon is difficult enough to deal with, but combine two socially unacceptable phenomena—in this case specialness and sexuality—and there is bound to be real trouble, including avoidance behavior. The mind tends to be fascinated by each taboo but is rendered inoperative by the two in combination. Heap one taboo on another, and the mind is boggled, or so it has tended to be in the past. Cool rationality, which might bring sound knowledge and objective reasoning to the subject of sexuality of special groups, has simply not had a chance. To emphasize this point, I commented elsewhere:

> The mentally retarded do indeed tend to be mentally retarded with respect to sex education—and this is one of the characteristics that they share most fully with the brilliant and so-called normal. Nearly all of us are mentally retarded with regard to sex; and many intellectually bright people are not even educable or trainable in this respect. Unfortunately, some of these sexually uneducable people are supposed to instruct or otherwise manage the lives of the retarded concerning sex.[2]

In spite of all the individual and societal preoccupation, sex has been abhorred, feared, hated and rejected. And for all the

---

[2] W. R. Johnson, "Sex Education of the Mentally Retarded," in F. F. de la Cruz and G. D. LaVeck, eds., *Human Sexuality and the Mentally Retarded* (New York, Brummer/Mazel, 1973).

sentimentality in our tradition, handicapping conditions* including advancing age have been abhorred, rejected and even ridiculed. (Many successful comedians past and present—Laurel and Hardy to Jerry Lewis—have done little more than imitate the retarded.) Aging is generally viewed as progressive deformity in a youth-worshipping society.

As a result of changing circumstances, educators and counselors have in recent years begun to exhibit a degree of boldness on the subject of sex. A spin-off from this development has been a relatively small but growing feeling on the part of those working with special groups of the need to provide appropriate sex education and counseling for these individuals. Special group workers have considered the entire matter, formulated philosophical positions and produced guidelines and even educational materials for their specific groups. At the very least, specialists have been declaring that their groups, whether physically or mentally handicapped or elderly, are first and foremost human beings. As such, they are likely to have sexual interests deserving of expression, respect and even accommodation. Progress indeed!

Still, my own basic work in the field, namely with parents of children in the clinic, has never permitted me to forget there is danger in talking of the sexuality of this or that group. The impression is all too easily given that there is something fundamentally different about both these individuals and their sexuality. Therefore, in my teaching and counseling various sexual behaviors and their significance are discussed, but not primarily with respect to specific conditions such as mental retardation, blindness or cerebral palsy; rather, these subjects are treated as common human behaviors having meaning to individuals within our particular social context.

I was interested to note that parents respond in like fashion. In raising questions concerning their own children, parents are likely to talk in terms of behaviors and their meanings, not about the "special" status of the child. Thus, it may turn out that the child is a bright "brain-injured" six year old or a mentally

---

* Tringo, J. L., "The Hierarchy of Preference Toward Disability Groups," *J of Special Education,* 4:3: 1970, 295-306.

retarded sixteen year old. But the questions are the same: "What should I do about my child's masturbating?" "If my child uses these obscene words. . . ." "When should a father stop kissing his child?" "Is it bad for a mother to tussle with her son?" With regard to masturbation, for example, what the parent wants to know is something about the significance of the behavior—how he should react to it, whether the child can be expected to learn the concept of time and place and how to avoid or discourage the behavior in inappropriate places without making a great issue of it. There is a quick shift from moral and mental health views to very practical levels. These are not basically questions about handicapping conditions. They are questions about our knowledge of the meaning of sexual behaviors, about developmental levels with special reference to social awareness and about how to help the child to live in a sexually conflicted society which is both for and against sex, both sex-centric and sex-rejecting.

The clinic approach to the sex education and counseling of parents about the sexuality of their children may be of interest because it seems efficient and reasonably effective.

1. The parents receive basic classroom instruction on topics which past experience has demonstrated to be of greatest common interest. Perhaps only five or six topics are dealt with because of time limitations (about 30 minutes). But these are intended to serve as a model for informed, objective confrontation with and analysis of other subjects as well. The underlying theme of the presentation can be stated in the following terms: Since most common sexual and sex-related behaviors are in themselves harmless or, perhaps, even beneficial, why make needless problems of them?

2. A challenge is presented as follows (this challenge is more fully discussed in Chapter 4): It used to be the responsibility of the parent or professional person to eliminate sexual expression among most special group members, as among children. Today, however, there is not just one possibility, there are three: (a) still try to eliminate sexual expression; (b) to tolerate or even accommodate it; or (c) to cultivate it as one might cultivate

other personality resources such as intelligence, artistic ability or sports aptitude. Which, I ask parents, is your choice? Most seem willing to accept the challenge and try to think out just where they stand. Certainly there has been a shift to choice (b); but a few people opt for (c).

3. Questions are then invited. The gathering begins as instruction and ends in effect as small group counseling and then individual counseling. Parents always bring up sex-related problems of their children at this point. Pedagogy shifts to counseling, with other parents spontaneously becoming involved as they have experiences to recount, questions to raise, solutions to propose. If the person who posed the problem does not seem to be applying information presented earlier, others call this to his attention. Sometimes, within minutes, there are fascinating changes in outlook and reassessment of situations. Factual misconceptions and moral confusions often quickly disappear as people begin to deal objectively with facts, specific situations and the possible meanings of behavior. Parents who do not have the time or inclination to bring up problems in the group come forward for a few minutes of counseling at the end.

Skimpy as this sex education and counseling are with respect to time and non-specific as they are concerning the special category the children are considered to be in, parents have undergone measurable attitude changes as a result of this program. An unpublished semantic differential test of sex attitudes, developed by Bruce Fretz* with my help and with support from the National Institute of Mental Health, was administered to parents a week before and again a week after they attended one such session. A number of statistically significant changes were found even though my total time with the parents was less than fifty minutes and the number of subjects was small (about 30).

Over the years, I have been impressed by the response of these parents. There have been hundreds of them now, and they represent something of a cross-section of our society, socioeconomically and educationally. Even in the early years, only

---

* Dr. Fretz is a professor in the Psychology Department of the University of Maryland.

occasionally did a parent become upset by my bluntly presented information and discussion which unavoidably often set traditional views topsy-turvy. My distinct impression is that professionals have been underestimating the public. School administrators, teachers, physicians and politicians tend to feel the need to protect the public from the realities of sex.

To put my impression to an informal test, I recently made an especially blunt, factual, non-moralizing presentation, put forward the foregoing challenge and counseled a few people who raised questions about their children. Then the next week, I told them that I had intentionally been very frank and blunt, and in the problem analysis period had confronted them rather starkly with their views and options: "So you caught your daughter masturbating and let her know that this was very bad behavior. Are you against pleasure? No? Then why just this pleasure?" "Your child drew this nude picture? Good quality for a six year old. You prefer that he leave the sexual parts out? Why? These are certainly breasts, but is this a penis or female pubic hair? Did you ask him? Perhaps he has some confusion here about sex anatomy that needs straightening out. He might repeat in school? Yes, unfortunately, the teacher's problem could cause trouble. Have you helped him with the time and place business in other matters? Then perhaps. . . ."

Now my question to the parents was what would they prefer that I do: (1) Adopt the professional person's usual policy of assuming that the public is not up to a direct, objective confrontation with sexual matters, especially as they relate to the young and special groups; or (2) continue briskly with my assumption that the public may be underestimated and wants the unvarnished facts and help in using them rationally. There was an immediate consensus for the second option: "We would like to look at things the way they are." No one could be egged into arguing for the former, although I pointed to certain merits of that choice. True, the deck was stacked to some extent by the circumstances, but the deck is usually stacked the other way around. And people who feel well supported by a moral conviction will usually express themselves nonverbally if not verbally.

I detected no support for the first option or reaction against the second—that is, direct confrontation with reality and objective analysis.

Admittedly, in this little experiment the number of parents was relatively small (less than a hundred) but it bore out my previous impression from similar experiences with hundreds of parents. In other words, I think that people in such fields as special education, social work, pediatrics and other medical specialties and psychology may find in the clinical experience support for a somewhat bolder approach in this area even though they may well encounter occasional objections.

Over the years, I have become increasingly impressed at the generalizability of what we have learned from the parents and children in our clinic to various special adult groups. As with children's programs, adult programs have only in recent years begun to face up to the sexuality of their clients and patients. Meetings and professional literature have begun to focus on sexuality of special adult groups. If the educator or counselor makes it clear that he is prepared to deal with the unvarnished facts of sex, the special group member is likely to speak up and to welcome such treatment of the subject. My own experience with the aging was further confirmed in the popular new Adults' Health and Developmental Program for older people. This program functions within the context of our children's program and frequently involves fun-type interactions among people of different generations—the children, elderly, young adult student clinicians (who work with either children or adults on an individual basis) and the adults who serve as leaders. In the older persons' program, the sexual dimension of personality functioning continues to be in evidence, and the educational program provided for them after the activity program includes a zeroing in on sex matters. According to Daniel Leviton, director of that program, people tend to speak up freely in the classroom sessions. Eighty year olds speak of the frustration and perhaps guilt feelings caused by sexual fantasies, thoughts and dreams and lack of sexual partners. They express the typical moral and health apprehensions over masturbation.

It so happens that while writing this book, I have become a member of a special group, the presumably incurably ill. A rare, progressive disease of the skin and connective tissues, of unknown cause, has resulted in considerable and continuing pain, marked loss of strength, coordination and general movement capability. My point in bringing this up is that sexually speaking, I followed the pattern which observers of the chronically ill have noted as typical (see Chapter 2). After an initial period, as symptoms intensified, sexual interest declined to a zero point. Interest gradually returned to approximately pre-illness level. Modifications in sexual technique were necessary (see the discussion on sexual intercourse and sex without intercourse in Part II) but gratification did not suffer. Having the benefit of a sexually interested, knowledgeable and sympathetic mate has made it possible for sex to serve as a morale-lifting source of enjoyment and pleasurable communication, as it had before. Under the circumstances, I have become convinced that improved sex education and counseling would be entirely worthwhile if it did nothing but help prepare people to adjust to their own or their loved ones' inevitable illnesses and infirmities. Illness is bad enough without being further complicated by fears and misconceptions of a sexual nature.

At any rate, my professional and personal experiences have led me to realize that being special in some way does not render people any less human, sexually or otherwise; that sexual interest is likely to be as important an aspect of life to members of special groups as to most other people; and that members of different special groups are not so different from one another, just as they are not so different from the population at large.

Part I of this book is directed specifically to special groups as they are affected by modern developments. On the other hand, Part II follows a pattern in which each sex related topic is first discussed in general terms, applications made to special group members as appropriate and finally, common questions are raised to pinpoint typical concerns. The perceptive reader will note that most of this material could be used with little change by most people not considered special group members.

As I have indicated, when it come to sexual matters, most of us—regardless of intelligence, health or developmental status—are in a special confused, conflicted, ignorant state.

Margaret Mead once commented that we owe a lot to the retarded because they have taught us much about the rest of us. We may realistically be able to generalize this idea. Perhaps when we can help special group members to live more comfortably with their sexual selves, we will have learned a great deal about what all of us need to know about personal and interpersonal sexual health.

--------- CHAPTER 1 ---------

SPECIAL GROUPS AND SEX

IN THIS CENTURY, handicapped persons, the aging and other members of special groups have been receiving increased attention as their humanness takes precedence over the "condition;" indeed, our society is thinking increasingly in terms of the rights of the handicapped. These rights, now claimed more or less successfully by and for the handicapped, have been in terms of meeting basic human needs for good nutrition and living circumstances, for recreational opportunities of various kinds, for educational opportunities, for the opportunity to be contributing, employed members of society and like everyone else, the right to fulfill their potentialities for growth and enjoyment.

Among the more glaring omissions in this general picture of more widely accepted rights has been that associated with the sexuality of individuals in such special groups. Until very recently, discussions of the rights of special groups have made little or no effort to take into account possible rights associated with sexual expression. Of course, this is not surprising because ours has been, and in many ways continues to be, an exceedingly sexually repressive society with respect to people generally and certainly with respect to special group members. It is fair to say that when handicapped persons have taken an interest in sex, parents, teachers and others have tended to view this as handicap or misfortune heaped upon handicap. With their greater mobility and other advantages, "normal" individuals have tended to find ways of finding at least partially satisfactory outlets for their sexual interests and needs; but the handicapped, with their restrictions and living as they often do in a goldfish bowl, have been very much disadvantaged in this connection, too.

However, a time of change is upon us and there are already strong indications of the sexual revolution extending to include members of special groups. It is our purpose here to examine the state of modern knowledge of and attitudes toward human sexuality with specific application to persons commonly categorized as "special" due to some handicap, disability or more advanced age. For purposes of clarity, let us begin with observations concerning the nature of what I call "special groups" and of sexual expression.

The Nature of Special Groups

It could easily be argued that everyone belongs to a special group of some kind, sexually speaking. To begin with, everyone falls into one of two special groups, either male or female. Children are certainly a special group having to make fantastic adjustments to a sexually conflicted world as they grow up. Little girls in particular, generally considered non-sexual until marriage, must deal with their very real sexuality while pretending for the benefit of adults that it does not exist. Married people with all the trials and tribulations they take nightly to the marriage bed are a special group indeed. If and when they assume the responsibilities of parenthood with all it entails, including the sex education of their children, they enter into still another realm of specialness as parents. Black people as they feel themselves perceived by white people and as perceived especially by white men are a special group. Homosexuals, saved only by their usual invisibility from loss of employment and perhaps worse, are very special. And so are swingers, single adults, doctors, clergymen. . . .

For present purposes, the term "special groups" has reference to those persons with some identifiable mental or physical handicap or disorder, or aging which needs to be taken into account for sex education and counseling purposes. Emphasis here will not be upon handicapping conditions but upon individual human beings dealing knowledgeably with their sexuality, whatever their condition. Thus it is hoped the entire discussion will be such that individuals reading it or discussing it will tend not to

*identify themselves with a group or handicap so much as with
fellow human beings searching for sexual understanding, adjustment and enjoyment within the limits of their wishes and possibilities available to them.*

This discussion will de-emphasize and insofar as possible
avoid labels associated with common handicaps, disabilities,
aging, etc. I have coined an expression which clearly reflects
my view on this score: "Labels tend both to conceal and
create the individuals under them." We are concerned here
with individuals rather than with handicap labels. What are
specific reasons for this? The label usually tells us very little
about the individual involved, and our ultimate concern is with
the individual. Examples will clarify my meaning.

While it is true that on the average older people are not as
sexually vigorous as young people, older persons may remain
sexually interested and active through their sixties and seventies
and even into their eighties and nineties. Moreover, just what
is meant by the word "older"? Behaviorally speaking, many
people are "younger" at sixty than others are at thirty-five. Then,
too, a great many older people would be sexually active (a) if
they had not been so thoroughly indoctrinated against this
behavior in their earlier years or (b) if society did not frown
upon sexual interest in the aging. Some need only sex education
and counseling to help them enjoy an active sex life—if they
want one.

As another example, the term "mental retardation" can be
particularly troublesome in this whole connection. It can refer
to a condition involving underdeveloped brain cells which permanently limit cognitive functioning. It may be due largely to a
lack of opportunity to learn middle-class verbal and other skills
or may represent developmental problems of neuromotor-
perceptual organization. Sexually speaking, the mentally retarded may range from high to low in reproductive ability,
sexual interest and activity.

In brief, such categorizing as "aging" or "mentally retarded"
—or, as we shall note, "mentally ill," "physically handicapped,"
etc.—tells us little about the sexuality of the individual so labelled.
Therefore, our concern has to be with the individual, regardless

of special group label or expectancies set by that label. Clearly, individuals in special groups are likely to be particularly disadvantaged with regard to sexual fulfillment and enjoyment. Still, many, if not most, individuals so inclined can be helped to understand their sexuality better and perhaps to incorporate this dimension of their personalities into their lives as other human beings attempt to do. Key considerations are societal attitudes (which are changing), knowledge of the existing possibilities and their implications, ability to communicate openly about the subject and willingness to explore openly the possibilities which do exist for the interested individual.

The Nature of Sex Expression

Animal species, including humankind, have continued to exist in part because certain behaviors with species survival benefits are pleasurable to individual species members. Thus, it is hard to imagine a wolf bothering to run down and kill an elk for the benefit of his species. He wants the pleasure of food or relief from hunger. Similarly, it is hard to imagine humans or animals going through their sometimes elaborate or painful courtship behaviors for such lofty goals as species survival. Personal gratification is the objective, even though humans may expand this gratification beyond the immediate situation for more distant gratification, such as children who will bring them status, support them or carry on their names. The evolutionary process virtually guarantees that individual members of species are born with strong tendencies to perpetuate the species by, among other things, eating and copulating—or more accurately, gratifying readily arousable appetites for food and sex. Societies have commonly evolved ways of channeling sexual expression in what are considered socially beneficial ways. In our tradition, the only recognized socially beneficial expression has been sex within marriage for reproductory purposes. However, individual gratification rarely confines itself to societal prescriptions, with sexual enjoyment being sought in numerous ways depending on individuals and opportunities. Our society no longer frowns so darkly on this fact and has been showing a growing capacity to distinguish between procreational and recreational sex. Personal sexual gratification and enjoyment are our principal concerns here, although parenthood of special group members is discussed in a later chapter.

Special Groups and Sex

In our tradition, even voluntary sexual intercourse has been feared and perhaps even dreaded for two tangible reasons: fear of unwanted pregnancy and fear of venereal disease. Both pregnancy and venereal disease may be initiated by a single sexual contact, and either can obviously have devastating implications for practically everyone, including individuals in special groups.

In addition to such tangible reasons as dreading unwanted pregnancy and disease, there is the traditional notion that nearly all sexual intercourse and other forms of sexual expression are intrinsically bad or evil. Certainly this irrational view has applied at least as much to individuals in special groups, though they might be incapable of impregnation and fully protected from disease. This attitude may be accounted for on at least three grounds: (1) As stated earlier, in the traditional-fundamentalist view, sexual activity is immoral unless it occurs within marriage and for the specific purpose of conceiving a child; even then it is not entirely free of the sinful for it is basically by means of sexual contamination that the believer is "born in sin." Strictly speaking, there is no real justification for sexual activity other than for reproduction. Large numbers of individuals in special groups, including the more elderly, mentally retarded, emotionally disturbed and many physically handicapped, have therefore been automatically dealt out of any legitimate sexual gratification on the moral grounds that they can't or shouldn't reproduce; ergo, no sex.

(2) A long tradition lingers that sexual interest and activity, especially masturbation, *cause* various disorders, especially mental deterioration, which is to say mental retardation and "insanity." Fortunately, in recent times this long-standing but entirely erroneous notion has been disappearing among professional people; but it is still widely enough accepted among the lay public, including parents, that it needs to be mentioned here as a viable factor in the dynamics of this situation. Obviously,

if parents accept the notion that masturbatory behavior alone or with another, or interest in "unnatural" sexual acts will cause or worsen mental or neurological deterioration, they are bound to go to any length to prevent such behavior. And they have. It is hard to believe the number of devices that have been invented and even patented to prevent masturbation.

(3) The third closely related consideration is that many parents will believe their children's misfortunes are a form of punishment for evil deeds of their own, very likely sexual transgressions. ("What did I do to cause this?") Such deep-seated belief that superhuman forces punish transgressors for evil deeds represents a belief in black magic likely to extend to similar notions about the magical means whereby the child's sexual transgressions lead to grave problems. Parents' or professional counselors' attitudes and beliefs in this regard almost certainly have a bearing upon their dealings with parents, children and other members of special groups. Interestingly, the "what did I do to deserve this" attitude is by no means confined to our own society. Hindu women with children in our clinic program have pointed out that one of the major obstacles in the way of realistic dealing with children with special problems in India is the enormous guilt feelings that parents, especially mothers, tend to have concerning their children's misfortunes. They are being punished for evil deeds in a previous life. As in our society, the resulting guilt feelings sometimes virtually incapacitate the parents in rational dealings with their problems.

CHAPTER 2

THE SEXUAL REVOLUTION AND
SPECIAL GROUPS

$\mathbf{F}$ IRST OF ALL, it is often asked whether there really is a sexual revolution in progress today. If the criterion of such a revolution is whether young people, on the average, and especially females, are more sexually active than they used to be and adults are generally more permissive with regard to this behavior, then the response is controversial. After all, both behaviors and attitudes have varied over generations and within social classes. One would therefore have to ask: More active and more permissive than when or where? Even the much heralded new openness in talk, literature and pictures about sex, including nudity, is certainly not unique to our times, as any student of literature or art history can readily verify.

Still, there is indeed a sexual revolution in progress today. This revolution, the existence of which is really not disputable, has to do with scientific and educational involvement in sexual matters. True, neither has progressed very far as yet. Wardell Pomeroy, of Kinsey group fame, has warned repeatedly that so far, fewer than 100 respectable, controlled scientific studies have been conducted in this very complex field. And William Masters of the famous Masters and Johnson team in St. Louis, has cautioned repeatedly that at present the wisest course is to assume that we know practically nothing about human sexuality. We have, he believes, achieved little more than a number of satisfactory tools for use in future worthwhile studies.

As for education, it is in an even more primitive state than scientific research on human sexual behavior. In the first place, science has not progressed far enough to provide a solid base in scientific data for education to rest upon. Lacking an entirely sound base in empirical data, sex education does well to be as objective and rational as possible with regard to considering what is "known" and especially challenging the common, often harmful misconceptions abounding in this area. Moreover, whereas the scientist, medical practitioner or psychological counselor no longer has to concern himself with opposition based on religious or "moral" grounds, the public school educator tends to be confronted at every turn with opposition or at least the threat of opposition from this source.

Unlike the scientist or physician, the educator or counselor is always vulnerable to protest from virtually anyone in the community who happens to dislike what goes on or what he thinks goes on in the classroom. Complaints are often not made directly to the teacher who could provide accurate information about just what is happening; rather they are directed to the school board and/or the superintendent of schools and the principal of the particular school. Often this makes the teacher feel as though the administrative and community roofs are caving in all at once. Then, no matter what is taught or counseled in school, should any sex-related incident occur among the school children, there is a good chance that whatever school sex education exists will be blamed for inspiring such conduct. This is true in spite of the fact that sex-related incidents do occur and always have occurred among children in and out of schools whether or not teachers are providing some form of sex education.

Thus, even though a major feature of the modern sexual revolution is that the field of education has been increasingly accepting sex education as a subject matter area to be dealt with, the fact remains that progress has been slow and spotty, though here and there dramatically successful by some criteria. As might be expected, a few universities and medical schools have tended to make the greatest progress—if continuing objective, rational, open dealing with the subject is taken as the criterion of progress.

The foregoing precautionary comments about the limitations of science and education at this stage of the sexual revolution are not intended to minimize the real progress made in both areas. Progress is indeed being made and almost every month new reports appear which shed new light upon areas of ignorance or correct partial or complete misconceptions; and clearer lines are being formed between existing knowledge and the much larger areas of our ignorance. One evidence of our progress is that we are more aware of our ignorance and are becoming better able to ask perceptive questions in the interest of further worthwhile investigations. Moreover, my distinct impression is that at all educational levels and in medical and counseling situations, teachers and counselors are feeling increasingly obligated to seek out and draw upon the best current knowledge of all aspects of human sexual behavior so as to present it in appropriate ways in the classroom and in counseling situations. Thus, just as in nutrition courses, where modern teachers do not find it necessary to omit discussion of vitamin E or calcium or to delve into the sacred food taboos of the Hopi Indians, Jews, Catholics or Zulus, teachers of sex education are avoiding "sensitive" areas less. They do not attempt to propagandize the teachings of any particular sacred culture, leaving that to the proponents of the particular religious groups.

The Sexual Revolution and Special Groups

The sexual revolution as outlined here has to do with a degree of change in societal attitudes which has made possible the unprecedented participation of science, medicine and education in somewhat improved understanding and educating about sexual matters. This development would seem to have significant meaning for some special groups. In ways, it may be viewed as merely a part of the more general revolution concerning the rights of special groups. Of course, just as human respect, civil rights, education and recreation for most special groups have tended to lag far behind those of the "normal," sex education and counseling of persons in special groups have lagged even worse. Sex has been objectionable enough in society at large without having it "rear its ugly head" among special group members where it has seemed even more meaningless, objectionable, inappropriate and even perverse.

Still, in very recent years a sexual revolution has indeed been making itself felt with respect to applications among special groups. Just as handicaps, illnesses, aging and other circumstances have increasingly not been viewed as deprivation of humanness, sexual interest has gradually begun to be recognized as a legitimate part of being human, regardless of circumstances. Parents of handicapped children had great difficulty in admitting to sexual interest and behavior in their children. Increasingly now, this is merely one more factor to be reckoned with as realistically and objectively as possible, depending upon the circumstances and the particular child. A new publication, *Sexual Rights and Responsibilities of the Mentally Retarded*[1] reflects this emerging view.

Ironically, just as pioneer work in special education is sometimes adopted in regular education because it works so well, certain sex education undertakings for special groups have recently become vanguard and precedent-breaking innovations for sex education generally. For example, few college-level sex educators would feel free to present a film in their classes in which techniques of sex play and sexual intercourse are portrayed in detail for instructional purposes. However, when the same material is presented as a means of helping handicapped persons achieve sexual gratification and enjoyment in spite of their handicap, "normal" individuals are able to perceive this as reasonable help for people with problems who might otherwise have a potential dimension of their lives unavailable to them. Of course the next step is for "normal" persons to raise questions: "Well, what about us? We need help in these areas, too. Why do you have to have a handicap to qualify for this kind of education?" The educator, with his administration looking over his shoulder, does not find this an easy question to answer.

------

[1] *Sexual Rights and Responsibilities of the Mentally Retarded* (Proceedings of a conference of the American Association on Mental Deficiency, University of Delaware, 1972).

So, to repeat, a revolutionary new attitude is indeed gradually emerging with regard to expression of sexuality among members of special groups. Not only is the fact of probable sexual interest being recognized, but very gradually, primacy of the individual as opposed to the group with which he identifies is being acknowledged. Let us summarize without pretense of thoroughness what is happening with regard to the sexuality of several special groups. These examples illustrate a new perception of each special group mentioned, but they also underscore the variability of individuals within those groups.

1. *Pregnant Women.* Pregnant women used to be routinely advised by their doctors not to engage in sexual activity for as much as six months prior to delivery. Moreover, sexual activity was not to be resumed for quite some time after delivery. Doctors evidently did not consider this restriction significant, perhaps on a par with some minor nutritional adjustment. Now, due largely to Masters and Johnson research, the entire matter of sexual intercourse during and after pregnancy is based on the individual involved, some women needing to refrain from sexual activity for an appreciable time prior to delivery and others being able to ' so engage safely up until the onset of labor. Obstetricians may recommend non-vaginal sexual activity during pregnancy when restriction is desirable, partly out of recognition of the fact that long-term deprivation at this time is a major reason why husbands often tend, for the first time, to seek sexual outlets with women other than wives. Similarly, many doctors openly favor resumption of sexual activity between mates as soon as feasible after delivery, because of the benefit to the relationship and because of biological benefits, such as early restoration of normal size and function of the uterus.

2. *Post-surgical Patients.* Individuals who have recently undergone surgery or are involved in some special medical treatment have been receiving unprecedented attention with regard to their sexual lives. Thus, cardiac patients are now much less likely to have their sex lives terminated and are much more likely to be advised on the basis of their individual situations. Some heart conditions are such that any even slight strain is likely

to be dangerous. However, some heart specialists believe early restoration of normal sex life to be an important aspect of total recovery, considering all that is symbolized by restored sexual response. Patients found capable of readily tolerating other moderate physical tasks can tolerate coition as well.[2, 3] Incidentally, as we shall note later, sexual activity need not be the athletic event it is usually thought to be.

People undergoing L-dopa treatment of Parkinson's disease are found to vary markedly with regard to incidence of libido increase.[4] These findings are of particular relevance to this discussion because they illustrate how early observations can lead to unjustified generalizations, such as the contentions that L-Dopa is a true aphrodisiac because it stimulates sexual centers in the brain, or that Parkinson patients are sexually activated by L-Dopa treatment.

In some surgery cases, the patient tends to feel permanently disfigured and therefore disqualified from further sexual activity. This problem is complicated by the fact that sexual adjustment following such surgery is rarely discussed openly, the patient often supposing that impotency is inevitable and/or that he could never be acceptable to a sexual partner. A case in point is ileostomy or colostomy where the bowel must be emptied without benefit of sphincter control into a bag carried outside the body. In such cases, there is a strong likelihood the surgeon's training has not prepared him to discuss post-surgical sexual possibilities with patients or to consider with insight the related emotional problems likely to be generated by the conviction of loss of sexual capability and what this tends to symbolize in terms of life generally. At least initially, the patient's self-image and especially feelings about his body are bound to be altered with a tendency to withdraw from people as well as normal activities

---

[2] G. X. Trimble, "The Coital Coronary," *Medical Aspects of Human Sexuality,* Vol. 5 (May, 1970), p. 64.

[3] A. N. Goldbarg, "Energy Cost of Sexual Activity," *Arch. Intern. Med.,* Vol. 126 (1970), p. 526.

[4] M. B. Bowers, Jr., and M. H. Van Woert, "Sexual Behavior During L-Dopa Treatment of Parkinson's Disease," *Medical Aspects of Human Sexual Behavior,* Vol. 7 (July, 1972), p. 88.

because of a feeling of freakishness. Ability to respond sexually can play an important role in re-establishing healthy, objective relationships.

Although sex is of negligible concern to some such patients, Dlin and Perlman have commented: "Sexual activity can and should continue after surgery"[5] unless, of course, it is simply out of the question for the particular patient for physical or psychological reasons. These authors report the case of an imaginative woman who declined to let her operation and her feelings about it destroy her personal and sexual relationships with her husband. "She prepared for sex as most patients did by emptying the bag and bathing. The bag was concealed behind a sexy pair of panties on which she wrote 'enter here'—arrow. The arrow pointed to the opening she cut in the bottom of her panties."[6] Her humor delighted her husband who found her attractiveness undiminished by her misfortune. These authors also point out that surgery does not usually alter habits of masturbation or petting, and that "the best guarantee for continuation of sex life post-operatively is an active sex life prior to surgery."[7]

Before and after hysterectomy, old wives' tales would have women believe that symptoms are likely to include nervous breakdowns, obesity, excessive hair growth and loss of sexual desire. These are misconceptions; the uterus and ovaries are not physically necessary for happy sexual adjustment. However, if the patient becomes convinced that the operation will eliminate sex drive or make orgasm impossible, there is a very good chance that sexual dysfunction will result. Generally speaking, unless there is such psychological interference, the woman merely resumes what was for her a normal sexual life. In a follow-up study of hundreds of hysterectomized women, eighty-five percent reported no change in sexual interest or orgasmic ability. About thirteen percent reported improved sex life (probably due to improved comfort and less anxiety) and about

---

[5] B. M. Dlin and A. Perlman, "Sex After Ileostomy or Colostomy," *Medical Aspects of Human Sexuality*, Vol. 6 (July, 1972), pp. 32-43.

[6] *Ibid.*

[7] *Ibid.*

two percent reported less satisfactory sexual lives, in most cases due to intractable attitudes toward their sexual mate. It is to be noted that this study was conducted by the physician who performed many of the hysterectomies; every effort was made to eliminate the common confusion between reproductive and sexual ability and to otherwise help the women adjust comfortably to loss of reproductive functioning.[8]

Individuals troubled by severe neck and back pain episodes tend to be troubled by both their own lack of sexual functioning and by guilt feelings associated with depriving their mates of sexual outlet. Following severe attacks, movements which hyper-extend or rotate the back or neck need to be avoided; but at this time sexual interest tends to be minimal. However, during the recovery period, normal sexual activity is likely to be resumed and to be an important factor in general rehabilitation. Physicians who are sensitive to the possible importance of sexual activity during this period are likely to recommend ways of making intercourse of the usual kind both comfortable and safe. That is, the male patient may need to assume the bottom position and be carefully supported, as directed, by pillows so as to avoid un-desirable movements.[9] However, the counselor may also wish to consider the possibility that safe positioning may be facilitated by utilizing non-vaginal stimulation, for example stimulation of vulva, especially clitoris, and penis by well-lubricated fingers. Also, patients can be encouraged to enjoy total sexual response without the usual vigorous thrusting but with more quiet and subtle movements. Resistance to such departures from pre-conceived notions of "normal" coition can ordinarily be overcome by the counselor's simply pointing out that such techniques are entirely normal and very gratifying.

Complete severing of the spinal column which results in paraplegia or quadraplegia destroys the usual prospects for sexual sensation even though lower spinal mechanisms may make pos-sible erection and ejaculation and occasionally, thereby, the

---

[8] John W. Huffman, "Sex after Hysterectomy," *Sexual Behavior* (February, 1973).

[9] D. Rubin, "Sex in Patients with Neck, Back and Radicular Pain Syndromes," *Medical Aspects of Human Sexuality* (December, 1972), pp. 14-27.

ability to reproduce. As noted earlier, the emotional overlay of such incapacitation may be devastating. For this reason certain specialists in this area have been emboldened to develop educational and counseling programs and the film "Touching" as a means of helping paraplegics and quadraplegics become aware of their potential for lovemaking. To film "Touching," a photographer lived with a paraplegic male and his physically normal mate. After they had become thoroughly accustomed to being photographed during their private activities, they were filmed while spontaneously engaging in a variety of general body, hand and body, finger-genital and mouth-oral and -anal stimulation which were obviously of tremendous satisfaction and enjoyment to them both. Perhaps the major significance of this unique film is that it will be followed by additional quality films and other learning aids for all special groups needing guidance about how they might compensate for their disabilities in order to enjoy sexual activity.

Conversations with paraplegics and quadraplegics have led to the somewhat bewildering realization that not only are most able to experience sufficient erection for enjoyable sex play with a partner if not for vaginal penetration, but also some insist that such lovemaking actually gives rise to sensations of exquisite orgasm even though the sensory connections with the brain have supposedly been totally severed. In one such case, a quadraplegic young man who had been sexually active and well aware of orgasm prior to his injury, insisted that lovemaking following the injury gave rise to precisely the same feelings of orgasm that he had known before even though, as he put it, "I know that this makes no sense neurologically, but I also know that I experience orgasm now just as I did before." John Money has explained a similarly remarkable phenomenon of erotic fulfillment during dreams of paraplegics on the basis of what he calls "phantom orgasm,"[10] just as Head* first explained vivid sensations in the phantom limbs of individuals whose actual limbs had been

-----

[10] John Money, "Phantom Orgasm in Paraplegics," *Medical Aspects of Human Sexuality*, Vol. 4 (January, 1970), pp. 90-97.

* Head, H., *The Studies in Neurology*, vol. 2. London: Hadder and Stoughton, Oxford Univ. Press, 1920.

amputated. In other words, the central neural counterparts of the bodily parts are sometimes capable of replicating and "experiencing" previously known bodily sensations.

Traditionally, there has been a tendency among both patients and their physicians to relate changes in sexual functioning to various medical conditions. That is, a range of diseases is assumed to affect sexual functioning; on the other hand, there are both conscious and unconscious indications of a belief that sexual activity has played some role in the development of the medical conditions. In a study involving nearly one thousand patients with internal medical, neurological, psychiatric and surgical problems in a general hospital, Pinderhughes and others expressed belief in a sexual linkage with the particular condition by large numbers of patients and their doctors. These authors conclude that in spite of the convictions of both patients and doctors, there is no reliable body of knowledge which substantiates such linkage either with regard to degree or circumstances. Moreover, they note that there have been no adequate studies of the actual effects of patient-physician discussions on this subject and that areas where the physiology of sexual and psychological functioning overlap, or have effects upon one another, are rarely known.[11] In other words, these investigators do not seem to doubt the involvement of sexual considerations in a wide variety of medical conditions nor do they doubt the possible value of physician counseling on the subject. The problems they identify are a lack of research on what relationships do exist and a lack of reliable guidelines on the effectiveness of sexual counseling. I have known physicians who discounted the possible value of sexual activity in the treatment and rehabilitation of patients, perhaps considering it of peripheral value like other diversions such as listening to music, watching T.V. or eating enjoyable foods. On the other hand, I have known physicians who were convinced that in some cases restoration or acquisition of sexual fulfillment, especially on a regular basis, could be a major factor in both treatment and rehabilitation of a variety of medical disorders.

------

[11] Charles A. Pinderhughes and others, "Inter-relationships Between Sexual Functioning and Medical Conditions," *Medical Aspects of Human Sexuality,* Vol. 6 (October, 1972), pp. 52-76.

In a recent article, Newton has summarized the situation:

Identification and management of sexual problems in medical practice concerns one of the most subtle and difficult facets of patient care. The problems are among the most sensitive and anguishing patients bring to their physicians, and at the same time represent an area in which medical counseling impinges deeply on individual and family behavior and values. Thus, medical intervention is often critical to the patient's entire well-being and to that of the patient's family.[12]

For those patients who wish it, there no longer seems to be serious question as to the reasonableness of masturbatory sexual release when acute conditions do not contraindicate physical exertion. Moreover, as with prison populations, there seems to be little question about the reasonableness of restoring or attempting to provide for sexual activity between married couples. On the other hand, little systematic attention has been given to the question of providing sexual partners for unmarried males and females who desire social sex. This will be a subject of later discussion.

3. *Mental Retardation.* Mental retardation is certainly one of the dramatic examples of a "condition" requiring individualized consideration. At the present time, more attention is given to sex education and counseling of mentally retarded individuals, their parents and others working with them than to any of the other conditions considered here. In the past decade numerous local groups, Planned Parenthood agencies and even the federal government (National Institute for Child Health and Human Development) have held conferences to explore the sexuality of the mentally retarded—their needs, suitable educational techniques and legal aspects.

Major revolutionary developments in the field of mental retardation have, of course, included recognition of the sexual component of the personality and the overriding need to think in individualistic terms rather than trying to make blanket statements about the sexuality of any particular group labelled "mentally retarded." As to the possibility for greatly reducing

---

[12] Quoted in H. I. Lief, "New Developments in the Sex Education of the Physician," *J Am Med Assoc* (June, 1970).

the incidence of mental retardation by discouraging parenthood by mentally retarded individuals, serious workers in this field rarely argue for parenthood as a right of the mentally retarded.[13] On an individual basis, however, there seems to be a growing consensus that sexual gratification is a right of the retarded. Understandably, workers in this field are aware that this is no simple matter. The chief job of parents and teachers is usually seen to be that of helping the retarded individual to live successfully in this society, and this society is not yet very tolerant either of sexual expression or of the mentally retarded—let alone sexual expression of the mentally retarded. Consequently, many are convinced that retardation and sex are simply not compatible, do their best to minimize or, if possible, eliminate sexual interest to encourage more successful functioning in society. This is usually a reasonable position to take considering existing hazards. On the other hand, many parents and teachers of the mentally retarded are becoming convinced that sexual expression for those capable and interested is too important a dimension of human life to be arbitrarily eliminated from consideration for this or any other special group. They therefore are devoting their efforts to helping the retarded individual to find sexual gratification in socially acceptable ways and attempting to alter societal attitudes so that private sexual expression on the part of retarded individuals is expected and tolerated.

In any event, it is known that the great majority of individuals in this special group are quite capable of learning the concepts of time and place and of confining their sexual activity to times and places in which they are not likely to run afoul of punitive persons or the law.* Moreover, it has been established that retarded individuals capable of learning to accomplish other routine tasks reliably can also learn to utilize the usual forms of contraception reliably. Existing contraceptive pills, intrauterine devices and new contraceptive techniques such as the

---

[13] S. Reed and V. E. Anderson, "Effects of Changing Sexuality on the Gene Pool," in F. de la Cruz and G. LaVeck, eds., *Human Sexuality and the Mentally Retarded* (New York; Brummer/Mazel, 1973).

* Fischer, H. L., and Krajicek, M. J., Sexual development of the moderately retarded child. *Clinical Pediatrics,* vol 13, 79-83, January 1974.

The Sexual Revolution and Special Groups 31

prostaglandins can virtually eliminate hazards of unwanted pregnancy without raising the issues of sterilization and the back-up possibilities of readily available abortion.

4. *Psychiatric Disturbance.* Recent research by Pinderhughes and others revealed the usual variation and uncertainty with regard to the sexuality of hospitalized psychiatric patients. Forty-five percent of the patients felt their condition might interfere with their sexual functioning, but sixty percent fully expected to resume their habitual sexual activity patterns upon discharge. In this same study, doctors involved felt it likely that sexual activity contributed to eighty-three percent of the psychiatric conditions as compared with twenty-six percent of the other medical conditions under consideration. On the other hand, the patients were far less likely to attribute their psychiatric disturbance or medical condition even in part to sexual activity. The patients were far more likely to indicate they simply didn't know whether there was a relationship. A major conclusion of this study was that in spite of the beliefs of physicians and patients, there is no solid information from which one might generalize the role of sexual activity as a causative factor in medical or psychiatric conditions; nor is there a basis for agreement as to how patients should be counseled concerning the possible involvement of sexual functioning or the effects of the condition upon subsequent sexual interest or ability.[14] It is generally agreed that to the extent that failure in sexual functioning or failure in the interpersonal relationships involved contribute to the patient's general feelings of inadequacy, absence of personal worth and involvement in life, sexual problems would certainly contribute to conditions with these characteristics and might constitute barriers to therapy.

It is clear that psychiatric patients and their doctors have quite different ideas as to the possible relationships between their disturbance and their sexuality. This is to be expected because, here again, the special group label tends to tell us little about a particular individual. Some patients seem out of contact with their bodies and other tangible features of reality. Under

---

[14] Pinderhughes and others, *op. cit.*

these circumstances, sex in the usual sense of the term may have little or no meaning. However, a patient of this type may be virtually symptom-free on another day and may have quite "normal" sexual interests and feelings. Severely disturbed patients may have strong sexual desires but may not be able to work out satisfactory means of expressing them, either in private masturbatory behavior or in heterosexual or homosexual contacts should such opportunity present itself. On the other hand, some psychotic individuals may function superbly as sexual partners, their ability to tune in this area being as remarkable as the highly developed golfing skills of some totally blind individuals.

5. *Obese Individuals.* Obese individuals are often considered physically handicapped with regard to sexual activity as well as being sexually unattractive. Years ago, a cartoon in *Esquire* summarized these attitudes neatly. A portly gentleman is leaving a pretty girl's room, remarking, "Oh, well, Miss Pennyworth, it was an interesting experiment anyway."

I am not aware of systematic research on the sexuality of the obese. However, it has been my observation and that of others in this field that many fat people have entirely "normal" sexual interest and capability—especially if they are physically active. Indeed, many generally sensuous individuals are especially interested in pleasures of the body, gratification of only one of which is fattening. Thus they may make excellent sexual partners if adjustments are made in bodily positioning and methods of stimulation. (Refer to the chapter on "Sexual Intercourse and Sex Without Intercourse.") The portly gentleman in *Esquire* need not really have gone away disappointed.

Considering the "unattractiveness" of the obese, it is well to bear in mind that what is considered attractive is largely a matter of social conditioning, our slim and Twiggy ideals being considered most unattractive by some societies. In fact, when freed of TV and other propaganda, many find less lean individuals quite attractive sexually. I have known men who preferred very fat girls as sexual partners, and I regret not being able to find the article in which an anthropologist describes how fat women "turn him on," the fatter the better. One physician* has made quite a case for the argument that fat people are fat because they have to compensate for insufficient sexual outlet by over-eating. "Don't reduce—seduce," he says; the need for excessive eating will vanish and weight may very well go down. At any rate, you'll have a happy, if plump, person.

Like other special group members, the obese are not automatically dealt out of the sex game by any means.

6. *Older People.* As people grow older, their sexual vigor and interest tend to decline. However, the extent to which this decline is psycho-culturally as opposed to biologically determined is by no means fully understood. Thus, traditionally in our society older people have either been supposed to lose interest in sex or to be considered "dirty old men," silly or intruding upon the prerogatives of the young. In his studies of people over sixty, Rubin concluded that most older people are so influenced by this traditional attitude that an active sex life is extremely difficult if not impossible for them—even though under the right conditions of freedom from this psychological oppression, sexual enjoyment might be a significant dimension of life in advanced years. (He dedicated his book: "To Hugo Gernsback, at eighty.")[15] Similarly, Masters and Johnson were so impressed by the sexual vigor of some of their subjects between sixty-five and ninety, they concluded that the only prerequisites for continuing sexual activity are reasonable physical health and an interested partner. Indeed, Masters tells the story of the ninety-three-year-old man who came to him complaining that he could only "do it twice now." "You mean twice a month?" asked Masters. "No, I mean that I can only do it twice a week now," said the old man. Taken aback by this sad story, Dr. Masters sent him off with the assurance that he was doing very well and that many a man half his age would be delighted to do as well.

The extent to which psycho-cultural influences may determine

---

* Scheimann, E., "Thin is Beautiful, but Plump is Sexier," *Forum,* July 1972.

[15] I. Rubin, *Sexual Life After Sixty* (New York: Basic Books, 1965).

sexual interest through the years is illustrated by the traditional Chinese. For example, one of my Chinese students, a young woman, studied the issues related to the legalizing of prostitution and concluded that under present circumstances, the legalization of prostitution in the United States makes a great deal of sense today. In an experimental state of mind she outlined her conclusions to her sexually conservative mother who had grown up in China. At first, her mother was shocked that her daughter would openly speak to her about sexual matters, this being considered improper for females. Then, to the complete surprise of her daughter, she became quite enthusiastic about the possibilities for wives to be able to line up safe prostitutes for their husbands. It became clear that sex is something that wives are expected to tolerate from their husbands even though it is unpleasant and perhaps painful. Therefore, it would be a tremendous relief to turn this distasteful duty over to an employee. Further inquiry on the part of the student led her to realize that this attitude was not by any means confined to her mother but rather represented an entire cultural view. "Well, what about you and people of your generation in this country, for example?" I asked. She answered that she and her fiancé had discussed this in great detail and were in complete agreement that sexual enjoyment is a fifty-fify proposition between male and female. She made it clear that the Chinese sexual tradition for females was coming to an end with her generation in her family.

Of course it will take time, but one aspect of the sexual revolution certainly has to do with a growing awareness on the part of older people and professional individuals working with them that the hunger for physical closeness and possibly sexual fulfillment is a part of being human throughout life and is not to be denied by an arbitrary age limit. For whatever reasons of biology and/or psychocultural influences, many older individuals will continue to lose interest in sex perhaps gradually, perhaps more abruptly; and some will report being relieved that they have been dealt out of this more or less frustrating game. Such individuals should not be goaded into further frustration and perhaps unhappiness by being led to believe that lack of sexual interest is evidence of failure on their part. Although the door is opening, there is no law which says that all must use it.

CHAPTER 3

"NORMALITY" AS A SEX PROBLEM*

Quiz: Are the following behaviors or conditions normal?
Coition without orgasm
Masturbation in adulthood
Oral-genital sex relations
Homosexuality
Necrophilia
Sexual activity at 80
Becoming a prostitute
Infanticide
Answer: If you answered yes—or no— or yes *and* no to all
of these items—and can explain why—you score one hundred
percent.

What is sexual normality? This question constitutes one of the major problems in the sex education and counseling fields. In fact, we Americans tend to be so obsessed with the question of whether we are normal that we suffer from a syndrome which may be called a "normality mystique." We tend to scrutinize ourselves, our mates, our friends, our children—even our clients and patients—in an effort to determine whether we or they are normal. Newborns must be examined for normality, even by their mothers, before they are welcomed into the world. We cringe at the thought of anything associated with our not being normal. Our bodies, faces, hands, minds, behavior in specific situations— not to mention our intelligence, strength and sexuality including

---

* An earlier version of this chapter (What is sexual normality? by W. R. Johnson and B. R. Fretz) appeared in *Sexual Behavior,* June 1972.

sexual behavior all come under constant scrutiny for normality. Clearly, special group members are likely to have more than their fair share of problems with the normality mystique, especially the sexual area.

Let us probe briefly into this whole question of what is sexual normality as a preparation for evaluating various sexual behaviors. By determining just what we may mean by the word "normal" we may be better able to free ourselves to think about and evaluate behaviors without unnecessarily complicating the whole question by making a problem of "normality." Five long-standing but frequently confused models of normality are selected arbitrarily for consideration. Let us look at each of the five suggested models to see what kinds of judgments are made from the viewpoints of each, and see what difficulties each produces if permitted to be the exclusive basis for judgment of "normality."

Subjective Model. First, there is the subjective model, illustrated by the Quaker saying, "Sometimes I think everyone in the world is queer save thee and me, and sometimes I wonder about thee." This model recognizes that each person can make independent judgments of normality using only an idiosyncratic basis. For example, both Kinsey and Masters found that men generally consider their own frequency of masturbation normal, be it once a day or once a month—but any greater frequency likely to have ill effects, and any less frequency likely to indicate sexual inadequacy. Generally women have, until recently, tended to judge their own masturbation, frequent or rare, unspeakably abnormal. Obviously, the prominence of other models of normality tend to limit the use of this model. One can use oneself as the measuring stick only so far. Thus, even though significant numbers of people are convinced of the normalness of their own masturbation, homosexuality, fetish, coitus-reservatus, oral-genital technique and even autofellation, in the real world this subjective model is likely to be overwhelmed by others and lose its stamp of approval. A major reason for considering this model is to remind ourselves that we often find persons whom we might consider abnormal from any of a variety of viewpoints, yet the person himself is firmly convinced of his own normality.

The strength of the modern "gay is good" movement is based on the homosexual's conviction that his or her sexual preference is perfectly normal. Conversely, and sometimes most disconcertingly, we may find ourselves adjudged abnormal for behaviors which we stoutly maintain are normal, at least for us. Writers on sex are by no means judged entirely normal by some.

The Moral Model. The moral model is perhaps the most definitive. Abnormality simply equals sin. Actually, what is moral behavior tends to be equated with ideal behavior more than what most people actually practice. Thus, if this model is the exclusive basis for judging normality, since most people cannot live up to an ideal of behavior they have to be judged abnormal perhaps in a rather extensive number of behaviors. If you are not a saint, you are a sinner. The fact that most people fall short of the ideal was one of the great messages of the Kinsey reports—which is to say that by traditional standards of sexual morality, most people are immoral. But this standard must be taken very seriously, for our sex laws generally derive from this tradition. This is to say that what is immoral is not only sinful but also likely to be unlawful. Therefore, as Kinsey and others have pointed out, if the sex laws of our land which are intended to enforce morality were strictly enforced, most Americans would spend some time in jail, very likely a great deal of time. And many do.

Moral judgments are not always equally indicative of normal and abnormal behavior. Thus, extra-marital sexual relations and bestiality are immoral and "sinful" and, therefore, presumably both abnormal. Still, in discussions on abnormal behavior, extra-marital relations are not included in examples of serious violations of normality, whereas bestiality certainly is. Interestingly, both behaviors are considered normal among certain segments of our population, e.g., among "swingers" and in some sheep-raising areas.

The traditional criterion of normal sexual relationships in our society has been penis in vagina with woman on her back, man on top, "missionary style," and ideally aimed at reproduction—all taking place within the context of marriage. A recent trial of an alleged homosexual at which I served as an expert witness provided an example of how normality, morals and the law become intertwined and confused. The prosecution attempted to require me to admit that I teach that normal heterosexual sex involves a couple lying as described above. In summation, the prosecution stated that to allow deviations from this method of coition would be to undermine the moral tradition on which the nation is based. He won.

So the societal conflict is clear and dynamic. Large segments of the population view recreational sex in various forms entirely normal. But the law does not tend to. Nor do most parents or officials associated with the law, with education, with hospitals or institutions where traditional morality tends to dictate sexual normality.

Cultural Model. It is important to isolate a cultural model of normality because this model can help one break away from his ethnocentric fixation by means of intercultural comparisons. In other words, if all you know is your own cultural ways and values, it will not occur to you that your criteria of normality are not based upon your humanness but upon your having happened to grow up in a particular society or community. There is necessarily a great deal of overlapping of this model with the moral model. For example, every culture evolves its own customs and from these are derived mores and morals which in our case are the basis for our sex laws.

Within cultures, judgments of normality are made by comparing a given behavior to the "common" behavior in the society. Thus, nudism in public is abnormal in the United States, but it is quite normal in many other parts of the world. Anthropological studies have revealed much of the incredible range of differences in what is considered normal in different societies, virtually any sexual behavior imaginable being considered somewhere on a scale between normal and abnormal by different societies.[1,2] Remarkable extremes may be noted. Jeff Cosnow found that the Kipsegis of East Africa require circumcision of all

---

[1] C. S. Ford and F. A. Beach, *Patterns of Sexual Behavior* (New York: Harper, 1951).

[2] D. S. Marshall and R. C. Suggs, *Human Sexual Behavior* (New York: Basic Books, 1971).

girls who wish to marry rather than become prostitutes; any child born to an uncircumcised woman is culturally defined a monster and killed.[3] Ronald Berndt studied modern cannibals of New Guinea highlands. On one occasion, a woman became angry with her male relative, not because he was having intercourse with a just-murdered corpse but because he was cutting the body up improperly while doing so.[4] Indeed, as Belzer and I have pointed out, although study of primitive societies has little to teach us about what is "natural" human sexual behavior, it certainly heightens awareness of human sexual potential and alerts us to how abnormal we must seem to most other peoples of the world.[5]

Of course, a main difficulty with the cultural model of normality is shown by the fact that although most of us consider ourselves aware of the cultural norms of our society, rapid disagreement readily occurs if we begin to discuss "our" cultural norms. In a large pluralistic society like ours, the "norms" are indeed elusive. Are United States norms represented by residents of Manhattan Island, Greenwich Village, Kansas City, Haight-Ashbury, Hollywood or Jackson Hole? It is depressing indeed to have to admit that Dreiser's dreadful *American Tragedy* still reflects normative sexual behavior of a large segment of American society.

The cultural tradition has given rise to sex-role stereotypes which profoundly affect sexual behaviors. Two obvious examples: men, who are supposed to be sexually aggressive and know or should know all about sex, are therefore profoundly ego-threatened if they cannot handle all possible sexual situations or must seek professional help; and the language of sex, which is not openly usable among nice people and certainly not between the sexes, can result in a sex-life failure between mates simply because they can't talk about it frankly.

The Statistical Model. The fourth model, the statistical, is primarily a quantification of the cultural model. By means of a

---

[3] Jeff Cosnow, Personal Communication (1971).

[4] Ronald Berndt, *Excess and Restraint* (Chicago: University of Chicago Press, 1965).

[5] W. R. Johnson and E. Belzer, *op. cit.*

sampling of the behavior of a given society, a set of statistics is provided on a given behavior. The Kinsey reports are perhaps the best known statistical norms on United States sexual behavior. Abnormality, judged solely from this model, is in terms of deviation from the mean. Disagreements inherent in using this model to judge normality become evident if we note that the label genius is hardly ever suggested for more than a top two percent of society; but according to Kinsey's statistics, over three percent of our men are exclusively homosexual. Therefore, a genius is more deviant from the mean than a homosexual and therefore more abnormal—by the statistical model.

The normality mystique of our society is very much influenced by this model. On the negative side, suspected deviation from the mean is likely to alarm people. Thus, when women learn about multiple orgasm and how many orgasms different women experience, they often worry about the normality of their particular number. On the other hand, it is reassuring to people when they are told that they are nesting comfortably somewhere within the normal range, as for example with regard to penis size; or that they are not so uniquely awful—at least sixty percent of other women masturbate too; and many, if not most, women as well as men doubtless have helpful, untellable, harmless fantasies while engaging in coition or masturbation.

The statistical model runs afoul of certain of the other models, as we have noted earlier. For example, the cultural-moral (including legal) models proclaim that there is a certain acceptable, normal positioning for coition. But if pleasure for the woman is considered important, the odds favor greater enjoyment for her if she is on top or in some other position; if pregnancy is being sought, on the average, success is more likely if the woman is on knees and forearms, buttocks elevated with the man mounting from the rear, à la vache (medical or culturally normal language, but meaning "cow style" in French) or dog style (abnormal language). And so it goes. In our tradition, masturbation is normal only by the statistical model.

The Clinical Model. The final model to be considered here is the clinical. This model usually purports to equate normality with health, including healthful behaviors. Among other things, it notes that a statistical or cultural norm, as well as a moral or subjective norm, may not be at all healthy in terms of the psychological effects on the individual. For example, anxiety is a statistical norm in our society and sexual abstinence is a moral norm for single people. Yet both conditions have debilitating psychological effects on many people. The criteria for normality in the clinical model include freedom from disabling symptoms, primarily stress, and efficiency in adaptation. By these criteria, the unhappy, the unsatisfied, the anxious, the self-defeating, the inefficient—these are the abnormal. The efficiency aspects of this model are important in noting that a given behavior may be efficient and therefore normal for one situation and yet not for another. Few of us care for a highly compulsive social acquaintance; yet when in an airplane, most of us prefer a pilot who will compulsively scan the controls rather than socialize with the stewardesses. There may be many other complications of this kind. Marriage counselors have not infrequently reported that mouth-genital sexual relations, though criminally abnormal in many states and therefore highly inefficient and self-defeating if one is caught, prove to be adaptably efficient for many couples in their lovemaking.

Clinical normality may also have reference to a disease or condition pursuing its normal, albeit, destructive or even fatal course. Thus, Leo Szilard behaved most abnormally when he recovered overnight from terminal cancer, only to die a few months later from failure of a normally functioning heart. Similarly, a post-menopausal vagina may undergo normal deterioration, cracking, and so forth, unless rejuvenated by estrogen suppositories and restored to normal functioning. Moreover, with appropriate clinical help, an eighty-year-old may overcome the statistical abnormality of having reached that age and, defying the cultural norm, resume an active sex life.

Finally, clinical normality oftentimes puts clinicians in the position of parading or seeming to parade as arbiters of decorum and taste. Mental health thus slides into Emily Post's domain. And the doctor advises on the degree of nudity permissible in the home; at what age masturbation is evidence of immaturity;

whether women should initiate sexual activity; what sexual language is proper; what kinds of sexual response are normal; and so on.

In conclusion. A number of conclusions may be drawn from the foregoing. One can hardly avoid noting that any behavior may be normal or abnormal, depending on the context in which it occurs and the viewpoint from which the judgment is made. The question of what is normal thus proves to be a meaningless quest, usually ending in, "Well, it depends." However, if one can back away from the Platonic notion that there is some ultimate reality lurking behind words of this kind, it is possible and probably important to consider possible courses of constructive action in dealing with the concept of normality.

1. Abandon use of the word normality entirely because it has gotten completely out of hand and is, therefore, anticommunicative. But this is like the common recommendation that such multi-meaning words as "frigid" be dropped. Words don't drop out easily; the very people who recommend dropping them usually go on using them themselves.

2. Define normality as a *word*—a word capable of many definitions. The user must then bear the burden of stating just what he intends to mean by the word in a particular context. The alternative is pseudo-communication.

Significantly, in recent years, thoughtful writers have urged keeping but redefining the word "morality" so it will have useful meaning. The point of their argument is that behavior needs to be judged on the basis of its consequences, with respect to the individual and others affected. According to this view, no judgment could be made about the behavior until its consequences could be ascertained—which is the reverse of the usual situation in which behavior is prelabelled normal or abnormal, moral or immoral, good or bad.

Judging normality or morality on the basis of personal and social consequences has been a very helpful approach to many individuals interested in escaping the confusion of the multimodel dilemma. On the other hand, it should be remembered that people are just beginning to get used to the idea that such things as playful experimenting with a mate, masturbation, etc., are very likely to be normal by this criterion. Group sexual activity, mate swapping, homosexuality, hard core pornography and sexual actiivty among children would seem considerably more difficult for most people to submit to the test of demonstrable consequences. Behaviors such as these will not soon be labelled normal on any widespread basis if prohibitions continue to be based on prelabelled taboos. If, however, such behaviors are labelled on the basis of their effects on individuals and society, they may eventually be labelled normal—if the label itself is still in use.

3. Be particularly cautious when the word is being used in its moral, taboo, mental health and decorum senses. True, it is no longer fashionable to believe in sin. But a long tradition has profoundly conditioned a societal view, in many cases backed by laws, which leads people to behave as though they believed in sins—or taboos, as we call them among primitive people.

Sexual behaviors are often defined abnormal, illegal or aberrant without rhyme or reason. The report of the President's Commission on Obscenity and Pornography illustrates the problem nicely. Intensive investigation by highly qualified scientists unearthed not one shred of evidence that viewing sexy pictures or reading sexy literature produces harmful effects in adults or children. But morals and taboos need have nothing to do with facts. The President of the United States felt obliged to disavow the evidence in the name of normal morals.

At any rate, those who are weary of the futility and backfiring of ritualistic prohibitions, of the negative emotional consequences of repression and guilt and of the difficulties in modifying behavior when the individual has no interest in or sees no real sense in modifying his or her behavior—for all of those, there remains the possibility of changing the question from "what is normal?" to "what are the consequences?" It may then be easier to determine when behaviors should be changed versus when consequences of behaviors might best be changed; for example, eliminating unwanted pregnancy by near-foolproof contraception. Whatever other benefits such a change in focus might have, it would very likely increase the self-acceptance and self-respect of many now burdened with anxiety and guilt over the question of whether they are other than normal.

The foregoing general recommendations about "normality" as a common hang-up and source of confusion would seem to have numerous applications to members of special groups, many of whom feel the stigma of abnormality every day of their lives. The only sexual enjoyment available to many is likely to take some form traditionally viewed as abnormal, perhaps grossly so, by one or more of the foregoing models.

It would seem that special group members and those who work with them, live with them and love them would be wise to look very closely at the concept of "normality." It is entirely possible they will find it useful—not as a guide to their own sexual behavior but as a means of helping them avoid being slaves to any arbitrary definition of what is "normal" in their own sexual behavior. They may be reminded that the "real world" about them does have and tends to impose standards of normality, however irrational or irrelevant, with a vigor and even ruthlessness that must be recognized and taken into account by all who would experiment sexually.

Recommendations

(1) There are some cases where, if the question of normality is to be raised at all, the subjective model seems to be the most reasonable. Just as with choice of diet within limits of what is possible and what is available, individual taste or preference is what matters and is "normal" for the particular person. All too often, people needlessly worry themselves silly over the question of their sexual normality—their fantasies alone or when with another, their arousal over words, pictures, etc., their "unusual" sensitive areas, perhaps including oral and anal, their desire to experiment with varieties of places, positions, techniques or persons. What is right for you is normal for you.

(2) If you have the good fortune to have a partner with tastes and desires similar to—but never identical to—your own, make accommodations and expect accommodations. Here the analogy is more like mutual adjustments required for happy tennis playing, or any kind of playing in which interaction is

crucial. After all, if you and your partner can't work out a happy eating adjustment, you can eat at different times or in opposite sides of the house so as not to bother each other with unusual or even eccentric eating preferences. Interactive play, such as tennis or sex, requires a degree of mutual adjustment which is usually no great problem if people will talk openly and frankly together. Unless a partner is being well paid for services rendered, interactive sex requires some reasonable limits as to kind and duration of some activities. Anal penetration, especially by a large penis, tends to be uncomfortable, unenjoyable or even quite painful to most (but not all) women. To insist upon this activity often may soon lead to your looking for a new partner—unless you are willing to reciprocate with an equally demanding, perhaps unrewarding, perhaps unpleasant activity such as prolonged clitoral or anal licking, simultaneous vaginal penetration with breast and clitoral stimulation for an extended period, or prolonged spanking, etc.

(3) Be cautious about letting hang-ups parade as simple personal preferences and therefore necessarily healthy by the subjective model. For example, masturbation is a perfectly healthy sexual behavior, but exclusive masturbation when other opportunities exist might well give rise to questions: "Are there unreasonable fears of sex with another? Or of communicating with persons of the other sex?" Similarly, might exclusive homosexual activity, when heterosexual is available, reflect an unhealthy fear or hatred of the other sex—approximately half the population of the world? And might aversion to 69 be not so much a matter of personal preference by the subjective model as fear of failure due to ignorance of technique?

In other words, it would be a mistake to use the subjective model of normality as justification for inflexible adherence to irrational prejudices or fears or for failing to seek out education and counseling which might expand one's sexual and social horizons and enjoyments.

(4) Recognize your personal preferences for what they are—subjective evaluations—and don't try to foist them off on others as being what they should prefer. This is not an easy recommendation to follow, simple as it may seem. (I have known

auto-fellationists to argue that all men should practice their art, even though the necessary penis length and/or back flexibility is extremely rare.) Virtually every writer of a sex manual or sensuous-person book has begun by debunking puritanic rules about sex—and then has proceeded to set new rules and ideals: orgasms must be simultaneous, foreplay must culminate in coitus, 69 is the ultimate, etc. The famous Dr. Reuben has lent a kind of medical normality to his subjective assessments (or imaginings) and has thereby made innumerable readers feel inadequate sexually for not experiencing things as he says they should. Respect the subjective normality of others as you would have yours respected.

(5) Be aware of the other models of normality and, in particular, don't get into trouble by ignoring the moral-legal models. Society tends to deal severely with discovered violators of this model. Individuals need to protect themselves and those whom they would help from needlessly running afoul of punitive attitudes and laws which can have devastating effects.

CHAPTER 4

THREE PHILOSOPHIES CONCERNING SEX EDUCATION AND COUNSELING OF SPECIAL GROUPS

T HERE ARE AT least three identifiable philosophies concerning the sex education and counseling of special group members. Brief consideration of each of these might well be helpful to those working with special group members as well as to many special group members themselves, for the philosophy adopted will determine the direction that education and counseling will take, if any are provided. These three philosophies may be identified as "eliminate," "tolerate" and "cultivate."

PHILOSOPHY I: ELIMINATE SEXUALITY

This is an extension of the traditional anti-sexual attitude regarding sexuality in children and the confining of all legitimate sexual expression to procreative enterprise within marriage. Therefore, there is obviously no place for sexuality in children. Special group members have tended to occupy a somewhat less than adult status even though chronologically adult; and procreation on their part has made no sense whatever. In brief, the special group member has constituted quite enough of a problem without introducing the business of sexual interest or expression. Moreover, the long-standing fiction that sexual stimulation is intrinsically harmful if not evil has led to a deep-seated conviction that sexual interest is best eliminated by any means possible. In this spirit, the sterilization of institutionalized mentally retarded was widely practiced, not to prevent procreation which was not often possible because the sexes were segregated, but in a futile effort to eliminate the evil of masturbation, that dire source of further mental, physical and moral deterioration.

Clearly, according to this philosophy, the goal of any formal sex education and counseling of most special group members would be to eliminate or at least rigidly control sexual interest and expression.

It should be noted that some advocates of this philosophy have not been basically anti-sexual in their outlook. Rather, they have acted in the conviction that some special group members can get away with far less in the way of deviating from social codes than most people, and that their only hope of making it at all in the world depends on their living strictly by the rule book, perhaps particularly with regard to such things as sexual behavior.

Still, whatever the motive of parents and others in undertaking to eliminate the sexuality of special group members, they have often encountered anything but smooth sledding. One young woman dearly loved and admired her mentally retarded brother who clung to his interests in pornography and masturbation in spite of relentless spying and persecution by his parents. The sister's persuasions had no effect upon the parents, but she did communicate her respect and admiration to the brother.

The elimination of sex drive may be a matter of desperation born of love of the special group member. The mother of a very large, tremendously strong but severely mentally retarded boy sought to have him castrated just prior to puberty, anything to prevent the appearance of a sex drive. He had not previously evidenced interest in sex or females but was beginning to do so. Her fear was that his social ineptness might make his efforts to express affection appear to be a sexual attack which would lead to arrest and confinement in an institution for the criminally insane. Her knowledge of common conditions in such institutions made this prospect a continuing nightmare for her.

PHILOSOPHY II: TOLERATE (AND PERHAPS ACCOMMODATE) SEXUALITY

This growing view tends to accept not only the reality but also the normality and perhaps urgency of sexual interest among many members of special groups. It does not see sex as something to be eliminated but rather controlled with respect to the social context. Holders of this view are likely to look in the evaluations for the meaning associated with particular sexual behaviors. For example, is masturbation where others are present an indication that the individual is lacking in social awareness, an indication that privacy does not exist for him or might it be an indication that the situation is so boring that he or she is driven in desperation to any diversion that might come to hand?

Believers in this philosophy are well aware that life would usually be much simpler for all concerned if sexual interest and expression simply did not exist. However, realities of the situation have led them to adopt something of a "if you can't lick it, join it" kind of outlook which seems to say: "All right, this strong interest tends to exist in this person as it does in most members of the human race. It may be one more complicating factor in a generally difficult situation—just as it tends to be in the lives of most people. But it is there and it is real; so how might the member of a special group be helped to express his or her natural sexual interest safely and enjoyably within his particular social context?"

The growing tendency for special group members and those working with them to think and talk in terms of recognizing the human rights of all human beings would seem to make it inevitable that Philosophy II will grow in popularity. I personally have been very much impressed by the shift away from Philosophy I in the direction of Philosophy II during the past few years. People always used to be preoccupied with how to prevent masturbation and both heterosexual and homosexual contacts and how to control co-educational recreation and other activities in such a way that sexual liaisons could be avoided at all costs. These days people are actually raising questions about and discussing ways in which special group members may be helped to incorporate sexual enjoyment into their lives without having to undergo humiliation or punishment.

Philosophy II is by no means a majority view. Still, no great excitement seems to be caused when a speaker raises the question of the possibility of coaching male and female prostitutes for successful functioning with a particular kind of special group member or the famous (and by no means new) massage parlors which include sexual services on request. How about providing sexual stimulation as a reward for enduring excruciatingly painful or tedious physical therapies required by some special group members? This kind of question is being raised by believers in Philosophy II. Patients who have tried it recommend it.

Thoughtful adherents of Philosophy II are aware of the difficulties associated with including sexual fulfillment among the rights of special group members. They are aware that in this sex-conflicted society, people have particular difficulty coping with the sexuality of children, particularly young girls, with the aging and with other special group members. After all, it is not easy for many to see in the pathetic wheelchair victim, palsied individual, emotionally disturbed or mentally retarded person the same high level of sexual preoccupation that other people often have. How would contributors to the crippled, ill and aged feel about their money being used for the enhancement of the sexual enjoyment of the special group member?

Thus, in spite of the rather obvious difficulties, increasing numbers of parents and professionals evidently believe sex education and counseling can contribute to the overall education and adjustment of many special group members. They are tending to adopt Philosophy II, accepting the reality of sexuality among many special group members—a reality to be dealt with rationally, knowledgeably and humanistically, if not enthusiastically.

PHILOSOPHY III: CULTIVATE SEXUALITY

This view can hardly be said to exist officially. But in the course of history, there have been those who have proclaimed sexual gratification "of the essence" of life. It has been perceived as basic as good eating and good play, and at the same time pleasure in pure form, perhaps tinged with the mystical and hinting of the divine. This predates Epicurus and has roots in the phallic worship of all early religions. Some now see it as having special relevance to certain special group members, especially to those capable of sexual response but limited in other forms of gratification in life. Still, many genuinely sex-oriented persons would reject any suggestion that sex interest is justified as a compensation for frustrated interests of other kinds. Rather, sexual interest would be prominent regardless of how many other gratifications might exist in life. It would be cultivated for its own sake, just as other talents are cultivated. The film *Touching*, concerned with paraplegic lovemaking possibilities, is perhaps the best known example of Philosophy III.*

Many people, if not most, tend to focus their lives on sexual enjoyment when they gain sudden access to it, as when newly married, discovering a lover, etc. However, the honeymoon ends, circumstances change, long-standing anti-sexual conditioning asserts itself and sex is relegated to a minor, probably not very happy, episodic role—an unsatisfied preoccupation to be preyed upon by advertisers and entertainers. Sex gratification may become an occasional, desperate, spiritless, perhaps guilt-ridden episode. This is not adequate for believers in Philosophy III.

Some special group members, usually with the help of like-minded friends, professional and otherwise, have made Philosophy III something of a way of life. John Money, medical psychologist at Johns Hopkins, has observed leprosoria in the Far East and in this country several wards for severely mentally retarded persons and a prison in which the philosophy of officials has made possible the adoption of something resembling Philosophy III by interested patients and inmates. I have observed something of this kind myself. Some victims of heart attacks have evidently facilitated recovery by focusing upon the pleasure available in quiet, relaxed, prolonged sexual activity with an understanding, cooperative mate. Psychiatrist Joseph Markey has helped innumerable people, young and old, to cultivate sexual

---

* *Touching*, Multimedia Resource Center, 540 Powell St., San Francisco, California 94108.

enjoyment as a major life resource. Furthermore, Markey has observed that some paraplegics and others, war victims in particular, have fled the frustrations of high costs including sexual living and moved to Mexican cities where their meager incomes make possible the necessities of life, including girls who are willing to help them cultivate whatever remaining sexual sensoria they possess. Sex may be a central theme and *raison d'être* of the emigrant, and it is one of the main things around which the men endeavor to build a meaningful life.

Flying in the face, as it does, of traditionally held attitudes, Philosophy III is not likely to be taken very seriously by many. Still, it is a real and viable possibility and is therefore included here for brief consideration. To be appropriate to this philosophy, sex education and counseling would not be merely accepting or tolerating sex as a necessary component of personality but rather would be concerned with cultivating sexual potential so that it might play the fullest possible part in the life of the individual.

In conclusion. Philosophy I ("eliminate"), based as it is mainly on the Christian-Puritan anti-sexual tradition, views the appearance of sexual interest among special group members as handicap added to handicap. Sex education and counseling are to be aimed at eliminating this most unfortunate, perhaps evil complication. Philosophy II ("tolerate"), which accepts the sexuality of most special group members and recognizes the right of each group member to sexual enjoyment, will almost certainly become an increasingly common view of persons in this field. Gradual improvement of sex education of parents and professionals, lessened adherence to rigid, anti-sexual codes and improved communication with special groups on this subject—along with improved contraception and V.D. control—will encourage the spread of Philosophy II. Essentially though, Philosophy II views sex as a necessary evil to be accommodated as gracefully and non-traumatically as possible; holders of this view would not intentionally arouse, stimulate or cultivate sexual impulses but would deal with them humanistically once they appeared. Probably without fanfare or much publicity, Philosophy III ("cultivate") will slowly acquire a growing following as people become increasingly able to give calm and rational thought to the question of what the ingredients of a good life are. Fishing, crafts, cards and checkers may be in for some tough competition as recreation for some special group members.

At any rate, these rather clear-cut philosophies do exist. Knowing this may help special group members and those who would serve them to make up their minds as to just what their own positions are—and why.

CHAPTER 5

SOME PRECAUTIONS IN THE SEX EDUCATION AND COUNSELING OF SPECIAL GROUPS

In our new-found and growing enthusiasm for providing sex education and counseling on a broad scale for special groups, we may overlook the need for a certain amount of caution in planning and carrying out such undertakings. Precautions have been stated or implied in many other parts of this volume, for example, in Chapter 3, in the numerous commentaries concerning variability of individuals within special groups and the need to not lose sight of the individual bearing any particular label. Still, precautionary thinking is so important in this area where emotions tend to be so strong, knowledge and objective thought so lacking and people so vulnerable, that a summary of some precautions would seem in order. Those which follow are not necessarily in order of importance nor is the list intended to be definitive.

1. The language of sex continues to be potent and frequently anti-communicative. Emotionally charged words may literally reduce cognitive functioning. The old principle, "as emotional upset goes up, intellectual functioning goes down," has very important and obvious implications for both sex education and counseling. In brief, what it means is that the individual who is upset by hearing about or talking about sex is simply less intelligent in dealing with problems in this area than when dealing with problems in less sensitive areas. Members of special groups who have been conditioned for many years to believe that

sex talk is dirty and therefore not used by nice people, that it is sinful or that it is a subject too personal to be talked about find presentations on sex very difficult if not impossible to cope with. As examples: a man with good sensory awareness but no movement capabilities in the pelvic region delayed sex counseling for months before he could bring himself to discuss the matter openly with a counselor; a mother could not inquire about the masturbatory practices of her hyperactive son because the word masturbation was so upsetting to her; and an older couple sought counseling relative to sex matters, listened understandingly, but upon being questioned gave no evidence of having heard anything that was said to them. However, it should be noted that a calm, matter-of-fact use of the appropriate sexual language on the part of educator or counselor usually does much to ease tensions and pentrate the langauge barrier.

It is true that for many people, a suitable, usable sex language simply does not exist. The "correct" medical terminology is largely in Latin and quite formal; alternative words have tended to be represented as "dirty." Still, most people can be led to realize that words do not really have magical powers unless we choose to invest them with such powers, and a more relaxed, perhaps even playful, approach to terminology can be encouraged. It is probably true that most people are more relaxed about sex words than they used to be. Still, the educator or counselor needs to be sensitive to the feelings of the learner. For his or her part, the prospective learner or person seeking counseling must recognize that if worthwhile communication is going to take place, sex-related words, even sometimes the less polite ones, simply have to be used.

2. It is difficult but most important to avoid generalizing either from individuals to an entire group or from group data to individuals within the group. Most people are all too prone to attribute the sexual behavior of individuals to their membership in a special group or, on the other hand, to presuppose certain things about the sexuality of individuals on the grounds that they are members of a special group. The recent literature concerned with the sexuality and sex education of this or that group, such as the mentally retarded, has frequently been

extremely valuable, but it does encourage the mistaken notion that individuals labelled mentally retarded can be expected to behave in certain stereotyped ways when it comes to matters of sex.

Children designated "delinquent" are commonly presumed to behave in certain ways sexually, but sometimes this is not the case at all. People in various kinds of institutions, be they universities, old people's homes, schools for the deaf, mentally retarded or what not, tend to be presumed to have certain identifying characteristics with respect to sexual interest and behaviors. However, when such institutions are studied with respect to actual attitudes, interests and behaviors, variability is the rule rather than the exception. For example, studies of college women have demonstrated that whereas some evidently have no sexual experiences, including masturbation, during their entire four years in college, most have some form of sexual release several times in the course of each year and still others experience orgasmic relief several times in the course of every week of each year, usually by masturbation. Similarly, in spite of the widespread preoccupation with sexual prowess on the part of a great many paraplegics, others have remarkably little preoccupation with sex and adjust themselves happily to challenges of life without sex. And finally, some elderly people strive to maintain and indeed do maintain a surprisingly active sex life. In fact, some observers have been so impressed by the apparent sexual interest of some elderly persons that they have suggested the existence of a natural spurt in sexuality in old age.[1] Indeed, for whatever reasons, some older individuals attempt or do put aside former inhibitions. Some who have counseling and guidance become more sexually active than at any previous time in their lives. However, such observations cannot be generalized. Many are evidently quite glad that sex is no longer a matter of much concern to them and enjoy freedom from the need to perform in this area. In other words, recognizing the primacy of the individual would appear to be of the essence in sex education and counseling.

––––––––
[1] M. E. Linden and D. Courtney, "The Human Life Cycle and Its Interpretation," *Am. J. of Psychiatry*, Vol. 109 (1953), pp. 906-915.

⋏ 3. Another form of unwarranted generalizing is that in which the teacher or counselor uses himself, his training and experiences, likes and dislikes, as the norm which applies or should apply to everyone. In such situations, communication may be damaged by either gross or quite subtle considerations. For example, the teacher or counselor may assume that his or her own awakening of sexual awareness in childhood or youth was quite typical, as were also the family and neighborhood attitudes, the inculcation of family sex attitudes, the dating, petting and courting patterns, the masturbatory frequency and conflict problems, the furtive preoccupations with sex in the course of a sexually unfulfilling marriage, and so on. True, subjective models of teacher and learner may sometimes match to a rather extraordinary extent; however, this cannot be counted upon because there is also a very strong likelihood that background differences between the two are almost beyond belief.

Some of these differences are evidently biologically based. That is, just as there is wide variation within the normal range of appetite for food, activity level, need for sleep and most physiological functions, there is evidently considerable variation from individual to individual in sex drive—even though evolutionary survival guarantees that the great majority of individuals do have considerable appetite, sex drive, and so on. We need not dwell upon the extent to which psychological overlays may contribute to individual differences which may again widen the communication gap between teacher and prospective learner. However, a few less obvious considerations may include the facts that some men find the odor of female sexual secretions highly attractive and stimulating whereas others find them neutral or quite unpleasant; length of tongue may make stimulation of the female genitalia, cunnilingus, easy or virtually impossible; limitation in ability to open the mouth may make taking the penis into the mouth, fellatio, difficult, painful or impossible.

4. It is so important to be tuned in on the particular individual or group being dealt with. Specialists in the speech field try to remind us that when we give talks we tend to give far too little attention to the characteristics of the particular group we are to deal with. The old story about the little girl

who wanted to know where she came from and consequently got a long discourse on reproduction by her anxious mother, who was then shaken to have her daughter respond: "I think I understand, Mother, but that's not what I meant. Betty next door came from Kansas City and I just wanted to know where I came from." Similarly, I recall giving what apparently was a quite successful talk on elementary sex education, including masturbation, to some parents. I later discovered that one of the mothers who had seemed most enthusiastic about the presentation, particularly the part concerned with masturbation, had not the faintest idea what the word meant. I had failed to give some alternative names and to describe the behavior in such a way that it would be meaningful to her. Fortunately, her husband helped to get things straightened out because she was in the process of persecuting a daughter for the behavior.

5. There are hazards of both over- and underteaching and counseling in this area. Oftentimes, the greater hazard is that of overteaching because the teacher or counselor feels impelled to round out the picture, to make sure that all information available is transmitted. Sometimes, intellectually mature and intelligent learners do want as much of the whole story as possible; they are genuinely interested in it as a subject matter and want to know about such things as historical backgrounds, specific research and fine distinctions. Generally speaking, however, the learner is concerned with a particular problem or with an answer to a particular question that is troubling him and really has very little interest in the subject as a whole, academically speaking. Thus, when the girl asked whether it was all right if a friend helped when a handicapped child could not masturbate successfully, she had the answer she was looking for when the teacher responded, "Of course it is. That's a very nice thing to do." The girl had her answer. She did not need a further discourse on either masturbation or homosexuality.

Oftentimes people are deceptive in the way they raise questions. Instead of zeroing in on the specific question they have in mind, they will throw up a kind of camouflage by stating the question in very general terms as though interest were purely academic, whereas they are in fact asking a particular question about themselves or someone else. In the teaching situation where others presumably are present, it may be necessary to answer in general terms so as to avoid embarrassing the questioner and breaking off any real communication. In such cases, usually the intent of the question can be guessed with considerable accuracy. For example, when the mother of a boy wants to know when boys ordinarily begin to experience nocturnal emissions or why the young girl is so friendly toward her father and perhaps snotty toward her mother or why husbands go to prostitutes, the teacher can usually answer in general terms which the reasonably intelligent individual can apply to his case. Sometimes teaching situations become so open and relaxed that people will raise personal or family questions. However, often follow-up private counseling is needed. In the counseling situation, the counselor can usually reduce the generalized question to the specific one intended and deal with it within the context of the particular situation.

6.   In few other areas of human concern must the teacher or counselor be prepared for such gross evidences of psychological conflict and irrationality. As noted above, the prospective learner or client may be in serious conflict over open use of the language of sex. In other situations he or she may be quite "foul mouthed" but in the more formal setting may be shocked when the necessary language is used.

Ideals of expected behavior are so firmly inculcated that people often do not notice blatant inconsistencies in their behavior. "Nice" girls may seek out romantic situations but reject the idea that coitus may occur in them. Needle found incredible willingness on the part of college girls to risk pregnancy rather than make realistic contraceptive preparation.[2] One young woman confided to me that she went through two traumatic abortions before she faced up to the reality of her desire for sex coexisting with her unreadiness for motherhood.

Typically, girls are expected to be sexy in clothing, mannerisms and seductiveness—but not actually sexual. Mothers who

----

[2] R. H. Needle, *The Relationship Between Sexual Behavior and Ways of Handling Contraception Among College Students.* Doctoral Dissertation (College Park: University of Maryland, 1973).

themselves found it impossible to live up to the Virgin Mary-Raquel Welch ideal of girlhood almost invariably attempt to impose this same model upon their own daughters, as though it were the most natural thing in the world to live in terms of both ideals. Virtually all middle-class children grow up trying to work out personal adjustments to a world in which sex is obviously both worshipped and rejected.

It would be a serious mistake indeed for the educator or counselor to suppose that the situation is any different with regard to special groups or those working with them. People striving for improved, happier living for special group members have typically fought their sexuality and have been irrational concerning its consequences, all the way from self-stimulation onward. In fact, in some ways the situation is likely to be even worse with regard to special groups. A physician recently complained that he had just delivered a fifth child of a twenty-two-year-old severely retarded woman who was totally uninterested in her children and incapable of taking care of them, who wanted to be sterilized, whose parents wanted her to be sterilized so they would not have more children to take care of, and whose state permitted sterilization in such circumstances to avoid still another public burden—but whose colleagues in the hospital forbade sterilization because it would deprive her of her female obligation to be fruitful.

Happily, it has been my experience and that of many others working in this general field that more and more people, including parents and teachers, are increasingly able to perceive the incongruities and irrationality of many traditional attitudes toward the sexuality of special groups and to strive courageously toward greater objectivity and rationality.

7. It is a mistake for the educator or counselor to be overconfident with regard to his "knowledge" of human sexual behavior generally, and especially that of special group members. It is well to bear in mind that scientific research and education in this field are just now becoming respectable, and a degree of courage if not downright rashness is still required of those who are willing to brave the opposition and ridicule still commonly associated with working in this field. Under these condi-

tions, it should be remembered that we have not really progressed very far in building a solid base of knowledge concerning human sexual behavior, including that of special group members. People who are overly confident of their knowledge in this field often complicate matters by underestimating variability in human sexual response, attributing sexual inadequacies to psychological factors or oversimplifying or overcomplicating the role of sexual considerations in a problem situation. People at the forefront of knowledge in this area, people like Wardell Pomeroy and William Masters, never tire of warning people that scientific research on sexuality is just getting started and that it would be a mistake to be overly confident about what we think we know about it.

8. It is hazardous to presuppose either an entirely physical or psychological cause for sexual inadequacy or dysfunction. In recent years there has been a widespread tendency to attribute such sexual problems to psychological factors based on poor attitudes, ignorance, fear or anti-sexual conditioning. True, Masters and Johnson and others have established that psychological problems tend to lie at the root or at least to be important factors in most cases of sexual inadequacy, particularly on the part of the male. Thorough physical examinations are the first step in sex therapy. No amount of attitudinal reeducation or training in verbal and nonverbal communication skills is going to cure the woman who needs medical correction of some physical problem. Minor surgery may be required for satisfactory clitoral response; estrogen treatment may be essential for restoration of vaginal functioning in the post-menopausal woman. Allergic reactions have been known to block reaching climax. The prominence of psychological and communication factors in sex-related problems should not, therefore, obscure the possibility of very real physical problems which require attention before successful treatment can be expected.

9. It is a good idea to know something about the sex laws in your state and whether they are enforced harshly, leniently or not at all. Our laws derive from a tradition in which sex is equated with sin; and sexual expression, except under very narrowly prescribed conditions, is likely to be against the law.

The laws of several states tend to be so absurd with regard to efforts to regulate sexual behavior that many of them are not taken very seriously anymore—but under certain circumstances they may be. Generally speaking, counselors, including clergymen, who recommend to couples that they experiment with different sexual techniques do not get into trouble on grounds of, in effect, recommending that local "sodomy" statutes be violated, but they could.

It is still commonplace for parents and other citizens to blame any publicized sexual experimenting, group sex or rape among school-age children upon whatever sex education may be being offered in school—in spite of the fact that such episodes occur whether or not schools are undertaking to provide sex education. There is little doubt that educators and counselors of the young are most vulnerable to accusations of contributing to the delinquency of children and other such charges because the young in our society have traditionally been assumed not to be sexual; therefore, adults who talk with them about the subject are presumed to be creating sexuality within them.

10. People who teach and counsel in the sex field are sometimes tempted to see only the sexual elements in situations. Actually, the sexual elements may be minor considerations in the total picture. Two very short examples may help to make this point:

Case 1. After very detailed discussion of a family situation with the mother, the counselor concluded that the solution lay in getting the woman to focus more upon her own needs for life satisfactions. She stressed her need to provide more for her own privacy, her love and sex life with her husband. The counselor recommended that she simply insist on turning her three children over to baby sitters on a regular basis. Now it was true that the family circumstances had reduced both parents, particularly the mother, to a chronic state of desperation, involving trying to serve the family and making virtually no allowance for personal relief or gratifications. However, the happy solution of the counselor did not take into account the severe hyperactivity complicated by near deafness and partial blindness of one of the children. This child was in a state of confusion and wild panic much of the time and was being rejected and punished because her problems were inadequately recognized. She kept the home and school in a state of turmoil and was unmanageable by ordinary baby sitters.

Actually, before anything else could succeed, the disturbed child had to have better medical attention. Years of accumulation of wax in her ears had gone undetected by her pediatrician; she was not being helped in a satisfactory way to adjust to the sudden gross improvement in her vision; and her hyperactivity was being dealt with quite unrealistically. When steps were taken to get at these matters, placing the child in a school where effective help rather than punishment was viewed as the best approach, and when appropriate medical attention was provided, there was hope for family therapy. With the benefit of effective professional help, the way was paved for a better life for the entire family, including sexual gratification on the part of the parents.

Case 2. A woman sought help because of her uncontrollable eating which had led to what she considered to be very excessive fatness. She considered this the major factor in her husband's apparent loss of interest in her, sexually and otherwise. Previous efforts to help her had focused upon the compulsive eating and the improvement of appearance to make her more attractive to the husband. The request was specifically for hypnotic suggestions which would bring preoccupation with the refrigerator to a halt.

Detailed discussion, however, revealed a great deal more to the case than loss of figure and sex appeal. It seemed that menopause and a hysterectomy followed by the loss of ability to continue the very responsible job which she had held for many years and the departure of her two sons into military service had left her with only her husband as the basis for close interpersonal relationships. The husband's rejection of her fit into a pattern of bizarre behavior on his part which began shortly after an occasion when he passed out while cutting the lawn on a very hot day. These events together had suddenly reduced her from being an active, highly responsible and contributing member of society and a key person in her family to life in a vacuum with a brain-injured, considerably disoriented husband. Food seemed the only way to fill the void. Her busy life and early training had made it possible for her to have a full and very happy life with a minimum of sexual activity with her husband over the years. This arrangement had apparently been acceptable to him as well, since their backgrounds were similar and demands on their time evidently made their rare sexual unions entirely satisfactory to them both.

Counseling of this woman was directed at helping her to recognize the husband's problem for what it was, to seek medical help for it and to find ways in addition to eating to make life enjoyable and worthwhile. Under the circumstances, sex played a small part in the entire quite successful readjustment.

11. In addition to those individuals who for one reason or another are possessed of low sex drive and interest and those who, because of intensive anti-sexual conditioning, are repelled by the entire subject, there is a third group which requires special consideration. This group is likely to pose something of a problem to the sex educator or counselor because they may be well informed on the subject of sex, quite relaxed about it, but lacking a feeling of urgency, deprivation, desperation or what not with regard to gratification in this particular area. The teacher or counselor may not be well prepared for a confrontation with highly rational, highly realistic members of special groups who view sex not as a need but as something desired, granted the right circumstances. If they are not up to sexual activity, if arousal is unduly slow or difficult, if erection is not readily achieved or achievable at all or if what has to be gone through to achieve some sexual gratification seems too much, they simply would prefer to devote that time and energy to something else. Such philosophically minded individuals are probably best left to themselves and not pushed or badgered to need something they would like but are content to forego.

12. And finally, there are those individuals who because of disability, age or other factors, experience a decline in sexual drive and interest—and are so happy and so relieved! Almost all of their lives their sexuality has meant nothing but trouble, distraction and frustration. What a relief at last, as so many of

them put it, "that doesn't bother me anymore." No longer being a slave to love may be most rewarding.

In brief, there are many reasons for using caution in providing sex education and counseling if the prime objectives of such undertakings are to meet real needs of individuals. The educator or counselor is bound to be interested in and impressed by the need to consider sex-related matters with many special group members. However, caution with regard to both identifying and approaching specific problems is likely to pay off in terms of meeting real needs and avoiding the creation of new problems.

PART II

SOME QUESTIONS AND ANSWERS CONCERNING COMMON DEVELOPMENTAL AND OTHER SEXUAL BEHAVIORS

INTRODUCTION

THE SUBJECTS CONSIDERED here are not intended to constitute the coverage of a complete sex manual. The questions posed seem to be among those that have special relevance to special groups, but not all questions are of concern to all such groups. For example, dating, V.D. and marriage have little immediate relevance for the young special group member, but they may have within a few years. On the other hand, injured, ill or aged adults may not be concerned with circumcision or developmental events such as menstruation and wet dreams, but they may be very much concerned with questions relating to intercourse or sex without intercourse.

It has seemed reasonable to approach the subject in developmental terms, starting with questions of special concern in childhood and progressing through the years. Of course, some questions have fairly obvious application throughout life rather than at any one stage, for example, nudity, masturbation and sex play. In one way or another, virtually all of the questions and their answers have important implications for the entire life cycle. That is, attitudes and knowledge concerning sexual behaviors acquired earlier in life are likely to have enormous implications for attitudes, knowledge and behaviors later in life. Sexual difficulties encountered by special group members in adulthood may very well stem not so much from injury, illness or aging as from persisting misconceptions which frustrate current adaptation or adjustment. For example, an eighty-year-old woman recently complained that she continues to be bothered by sexual feelings, fantasies and dreams but can do nothing about them. When asked why she doesn't masturbate for relief if not enjoyment, she protested her early indoctrination that doing so would weaken her. Similarly, people find it difficult to "pleasure" each other by means of sensuous bodily stimulation. They are often helped to understand their feelings when they learn of the naturalness of physical contact and sex play in the early years but also of the extent to which our society has traditionally rejected and punished such activity in the young. In brief, many adults would benefit from a reading of current information about behaviors more commonly associated with the earlier years.

It is hoped that the special group member or individual concerned with helping him or her will recognize the introductory nature of the information presented here. Quality literature, films and tapes which go into greater detail are increasingly available and should be used as a next step in meeting individual needs and interests.

CHAPTER 6

PHYSICAL CONTACT

P HYSICAL CONTACT, AS in the caressing and fondling of infants, would seem to be a basic human need. As the English-American traditions have demonstrated, it is possible for people to survive lack of much physical contact as they grow older. However, the common training which tends to limit physical contact to handshaking or, among relatives, a "peck on the cheek" probably deprives most people of a major communication and, perhaps, gratification source. In his important book, *Touching: The Human Significance of the Skin,* Montagu reviewed the scientific and medical literature on this subject; expressed amazement that something of such importance to human welfare has received so little attention; associated much sexual inadequacy in both giving and receiving sexual love with inadequate tactile fulfillment from infancy onward and concluded that communication by touch may well offer tremendous possibilities for improved human functioning.[1] (It is not by chance that so many of the sensitivity training and confrontation groups utilize touching of some sort as a major means of improving communication between and among people.)

With reference to our particular subject, there is evidence that friendly, loving, easy physical contact in such forms as expression of affection, comfort and play, including tussling, is developmentally and sexually valuable. These forms of expression help the child learn about his or her potential for nonverbal communication and sensuous pleasure. In our clinic program,

---

[1] A. Montagu, *Touching: The Human Significance of the Skin* (New York: Columbia University Press, 1971).

we frequently get handicapped children who cannot at first tolerate being touched, holding hands, having an arm around their shoulder or tussling on the mats with clinicians or other children. Gradually through play, such resistance is broken down. As physical contact becomes easier, the child is transformed both with respect to his self-perception and his perception of others. Lowering physical barriers signifies and encourages opening up and interacting with the world. In our new program for older people, we have already seen confirmation of our own and other peoples' observations of the response of these persons to warm, friendly physical contact. It is definitely part of the overall therapeutic experience.

The same kind of situation is observed in the "sex clinics" of Masters and Johnson in St. Louis and others. A major therapeutic tool for couples is encouraging communication between them by specific physical touching aimed at mutual pleasuring, as well as verbal techniques. Masters has commented that one of the easiest predictors of therapeutic success in overcoming sexual dysfunctioning is whether the patients are willing to gently massage light oil over each others' bodies. In effect, successful sex therapy in adulthood often depends upon overcoming the anti-touching, "keep your hands to yourself" physical isolation that is so much a part of the training of many children. Patients are taught to explore each others' bodies in great detail, to locate and cultivate areas of greatest sensory pleasure, in effect, to view sexual response as the total body response that it is.

Is it wise for those responsible for child rearing to create the reluctant touchers, nontouchers and antitouchers who, later in life, will have to try—not always successfully—to unlearn their unnatural aversion to touching if they are to function well sexually?

> Question: Is there a danger of overdoing body contact? For example, might not children become overdependent and cling to the mother excessively?

> Answer: The only danger would seem to be if the parents' gratification were to be placed ahead of that of the child. That is, the parents' excessive desire to hold and fondle

might conceivably interfere with the child's need to explore his movement capabilities, to respond to stimuli and to explore the environment. In other words, what is desirable is a reasonably intelligent balance between the security and gratification of physical contact and independent exploration of the environment.

With regard to the possibility of having the child cling and withdraw from the environment as a result of excessive fondling, the opposite would more often appear to be the case. For example, a mother reported being upset because her two children with minor developmental problems were "always hanging on to her and climbing on her and forcing her to push them away from her to get them to do other things." She wanted to know how to get them to be less dependent upon her and less clinging. My recommendation to her was to reverse her response to their approach. Instead of trying to push them away and into other activities, she was asked to respond by warmly embracing them and holding them while making no effort whatever to repulse them. Sure enough, when allowed to check in to home base to their complete satisfaction, they did not remain huddled to her indefinitely. Rather, they soon took an interest in other things and withdrew from her on their own. Discovering that they no longer had to struggle for the reassurance of contact with her, they sought it much less often and more briefly, usually only when tired, sleepy, upset or hurt.

Question: As the child grows older, might continuing physical contact be evidence of immaturity or lack of appropriate restraint?

Answer: Generally speaking, the answer is no. However, some qualifications should be recognized. As I have pointed out, in our own tradition free expression of certain emotions is systematically discouraged from a very early age, particularly on the part of the male. Even newlyweds are expected to "grow up" or are told that "the honeymoon is over" if they continue their expression of affection physically. Among the young there appears to be a very strong hunger for bodily contact; this may be especially important for children who, because of some developmental difficulty, are slow in responding to the environment and often experience unusual frustration and failure. It should be noted that among large number of adults who suffer from sexual dysfunction—the inability to respond sexually in a "satisfactory" manner—one of the most common symptoms is the inability to give and accept sensory stimulation with a partner. Deliberate stimulation of the skin by manual and other bodily contact is a major aspect of sex therapy practiced in sex clinics and by marriage counselors.

In the Children's Health and Developmental Clinic, we discovered many years ago that children's ability to accept and to give physical contact, to embrace and to engage in playful roughhousing tend to be evidence of emotional and social maturation, rather than of "immaturity." Moreover, in our newer program involving people in their later years, we have capitalized on what we learned from the children and have emphasized hand holding, arm holding, physical support and embracing between clinician and older person as a major means of communicating, expressing friendliness and getting support and protection during activities. The older people blossom out just as the younger ones do.

Now about the qualifying considerations: sometimes members of certain special groups, such as the mentally retarded who may lack social perspective, may have difficulty discriminating between situations where physical contact is and is not socially acceptable. We have one young man at the present time who has just such a problem which has threatened to get him into serious trouble. In the home and in the clinic program, he thrives on the physical expression of friendliness which he is not able to communicate verbally. However, he sometimes tends to approach strangers in the same manner of affectionate handshaking, patting and so on which characterize his contact with father and clinicians. Since he is large, heavy and verbally inept, people who do not know him are likely to feel threatened by his approach and to respond either defensively or aggressively. In close cooperation with the parents we are slowly making progress in helping him to distinguish appropriate from inappropriate behavior; in this case, restraining himself from indiscriminate touching and other contact is evidence of social maturing. Of course psychiatric cases often need help of this same kind.

Question: What about homosexuality? Does physical expression of affection give rise to homosexual impulses between members of the same sex, for example between father and son? When should fathers stop kissing their sons?

Answer: There are at present a number of theories which purport to explain the cause or causes of homosexuality. However, I know of none which attribute it to easy, friendly affection. It is not at all uncommon for fathers to worry about creating homosexuality by kissing and physically expressing affection for sons and to withdraw all such evidence of affection. The same is true between mothers and daughters. In spite of what some authors have stated on this general subject I have yet to see evidence that homosexuality is encouraged by such behavior. On the contrary, I and many other workers in this field have seen children and youths become very much upset and confused by their parents' and perhaps siblings' sudden withdrawal of friendliness and affection. Such withdrawal is not likely to be understood, particularly by those individuals most in need of affection and may be interpreted as loss of interest.

Obviously, one of the great needs of some special group members such as the mentally retarded is to learn to conform and to avoid drawing attention to themselves by socially unacceptable behavior. It is therefore highly realistic to be sensitive to the entire matter of time and place. Unless done by highly paid popular movie or T.V. stars, public embracing and kissing by males of practically any age is negatively perceived by society. Members of special groups are not well served if they are not trained to know when such behavior is acceptable and when it is likely to be self-defeating and perhaps downright dangerous.

Question: What about the question of incest? Isn't the physical expression of affection likely to give rise to incestuous desires when practiced between parent and offspring?

Answer: As with the case of homosexuality, it is presumed that the parent, teacher or other person dealing with the situation is in control of that situation. In other words, assuming that what people fear is true, namely, that sexual impulses are generated, the question is, are these feelings given expression? Of course they need not be, any more than the child's or unqualified adult's desire to drive the family automobile need find expression in actually driving it. I have almost never had a parent panicked over incest report actual incestuous efforts on the part of the child or youth. However, should this happen, it is up to the parent to set the necessary limits and if possible to help the individual learn what is and what is not acceptable.

Recently, consultation with a parent provided immediate relief in a family where the word "incest" was creating a great deal of difficulty. The mother was athletically inclined and enjoyed participating in the physical activity of her husband and two young sons. Somehow it was mentioned to the pediatrician that one of the boys had bumped his head during a family tussle which included the mother. The shocked pediatrician then delivered the mother a stern lecture on the dangers of incest and incestuous desires likely to be brought on by such physical contact with the mother. Somewhat panicked by all this, the mother then made herself conspicuously absent from such playful episodes; then the father began to worry about his influence in generating homosexual impulses by such play. The boys, who had school and other problems to deal with, were totally confused by this new development with their parents. The parents were very upset and at a loss as to how to proceed. A few minutes' discussion of these alarm-laden words, incest and homosexuality, helped the parents overcome their panic. Moreover, discussion concerning the obvious benefits of physical play among both parents (father and mother) and children helped the family to return to its former happy, unifying and communication-restoring activities.

In conclusion. There seems to be no evidence of damaging effects of human contact via the skin regardless of the age of persons under consideration. On the contrary, although systematic research has not spelled this out in great detail, there are indications that basic physical contact can be enormously beneficial to people, including those in special groups. For example, some paraplegics report seeking out and cultivating with their mates all bodily skin areas which may contribute to pleasurable and perhaps erotic buildup. We may go so far as to say that touching may be a basic human need among the young and perhaps the physically and/or mentally hurt. Among reasonably mature adults, physical contact may not be classified as a survival need as it is in the very young. But it may add richness, gratification and fun of a very special kind throughout life.

CHAPTER 7

NUDITY

ALTHOUGH THERE HAS been a widespread relaxing of nudity taboos in this country as well as in much of Europe in recent decades, the fact remains that we continue in the throes of a serious conflict between two major influences in our historical tradition: the Jewish and the Greek. In the ancient Jewish tradition passed on to Christianity, there was the strong obligation to cover nakedness. Thus, except under very special conditions, as when David danced naked around the Ark, appearing before others in the nude has been sinful and more recently unseemly or indecent. Generally speaking, the law tends to support this ancient tradition, providing punishment for indecent exposure. On the other hand, ancient Greek thought has also been influential in the Christian tradition. To the ancient Greeks, the human body was a thing of beauty ("imperfect" infants were routinely killed immediately after birth) and to mutilate it (as in circumcision) was considered inexcusable if not profane. Although virtually all our sexual morals and laws are derived from the ancient Jewish tradition, the Greek way of thinking has long been a contrasting influence, nudist colonies being a rather extreme example.

Nudity has become increasingly acceptable in advertising, entertainment and in the privacy of homes and other private gathering places. In many parts of Europe, nudity on public beaches has become increasingly acceptable in recent years.

In the United States, since public nudity is generally illegal, the major questions about it are concerned with effects on people, especially the young, in the home. Even here the extent to which views conflict is illustrated by the following examples: A woman wrote to a popular columnist saying that after her family left the house in the morning she found it comfortable to do her housework in the nude and wanted to know what the columnist thought of this. The columnist responded that this was clearly abnormal behavior and proposed that the woman consult a psychiatrist. The columnist was then immediately flooded with angry letters from women who said that they too found this a most efficient way of getting their housework done and did not at all appreciate being labelled mentally ill for engaging in this solitary nude behavior. The columnist immediately reversed herself, saying that people have different views of these matters and, therefore, it would probably be unwise to generalize about the mental health status of those doing their housework in the nude.

In another case, a well-known movie actor was arrested because of his family's practice of swimming in the nude together in their backyard which was surrounded by an eight-foot fence. It seems that his nearest neighbor could observe this depravity by standing on his roof and watching with binoculars. The judge's Solomon-like resolution of this problem was to order the actor to add two feet to his fence so that he would not continue to offend the eye of his high-climbing neighbor.

Finally, a man was recently on trial in Washington, D.C., because the woman next door complained that by looking through her window she could see him in the nude through his window. He was finally saved from conviction only because his lawyer persisted in raising questions about whether there were any place in his house where he could be legally naked. Well, yes, in the bathroom, but then how about the bedroom? Well, how about in the room where the hallway joined the bathroom, and so on, *ad absurdum*.

The above illustrations show the extent of the popular conflict over the subject of nudity. Implications for special group members are certainly apparent.

Incidentally, two things tend to impress non-nudists when they find themselves suddenly in the presence of mixed-sex nude groups. First, they are quite shocked by it all. Secondly, they are astonished to find how quickly they adjust to nudity and find it quite natural and not erotic at all. Some have gone on to point out that by this time they felt embarrassed for being the only person wearing clothing.

> Question: If nudity is a question of societal conditioning and expectation, why do some psychiatrists and other professional people go on speaking of it negatively in the mental health sense?

> Answer: Strong societal traditions do not die out easily. If anyone, including a professional person, is trained from early life that viewing the naked human body is bad, there is a very good chance that he or she will continue negatively disposed toward nudity in later years. It should be remembered that most professional people have not had anything resembling systematic training in sex education and have little to go on in their evaluations and recommendations beyond what they themselves were taught as children. Certainly the Jewish base of the Christian tradition is deeply against exposing the naked body. People steeped in that tradition, professional or otherwise, are likely to have very strong feelings about it. Thus, religion and morality, often backed by the law, wind up looking like mental health issues. Moreover, the mental health specialist, especially the psychiatrist, is called upon to make decisions in the name of mental health which might better be considered questions of etiquette or decorum. Questions about family nude encounters in the bathroom or partial or total nudity about the house or family nude swimming might better be viewed as matters of family custom rather than as matters crucial to mental health. Young children are capable of learning that what is okay in the home is not acceptable most other places. They need not be shocked by the discrepancy. Indeed, they may be more shocked or disturbed by great efforts to make the home conform **too closely to the community rules.**

Question: Specifically, what about nudity among members of special groups?

Answer: Members of special groups, except for those whose disability renders them incapable of realistic evaluation of social situations, are perfectly capable of doing what everyone else does, namely, working out some kind of compromise between their own preferences and the demands of time and place. Mentally retarded individuals, like many very young children, are capable of learning that they may happily strip off their clothes here but not there and also to spring quickly into clothing when the situation suddenly changes, as when visitors arrive upon the scene. However, in those cases in which individals have difficulty evaluating situations, they may need training that emphasizes the importance of being clothed in some way at virtually all times.

Our societal demands are complex in comparison with those of societies not in conflict over nudity. In some societies, requirements are comparatively clear-cut and simple. For example, in the Dominican Republic, nudity in the home and even in public play is perfectly acceptable until age six or eight when children begin wearing clothing; in at least one primitive society, young girls must wear clothing but women need not; in many, family bathing, even in public, is proper in the nude but outside this context clothing is required; and in increasing numbers of countries, nudity on the beach is acceptable but is unacceptable a block or so away where the beach ends.

In our society there is perhaps an unusual degree of adjustment required because nudity and various degrees of it are both glorified and condemned, and the individual may have considerable trouble in sorting all this out. Thus, one may have nightmares about being in public in one's underwear but may be perfectly comfortable in scanty beach apparel. Appearance in panties and bra may give rise to great embarrassment even though less covering in the form of a swimming suit may be perfectly adequate.

A few years ago it took a very brave man to wear knee shorts to summer classes on college campuses. At the same time, young women were wearing the shortest of shorts without the least inhibition.

In conclusion. So far as I have been able to discover, there is no evidence of psychological damage brought about by the practice or viewing of nudity. The relatively few special group members who, like children, need help in fathoming the complexities of our societal expectations are helped by consistency rather than abrupt changes. They may very well be less likely to run afoul of local attitudes and the law if their training is on the conservative side.

Nudity is obviously a natural state. But attitudes toward it depend upon societal conditioning. Since our own society is ambiguous and therefore conflicted on this subject, individuals, families and communities are also. Being unusually vulnerable, many members of special groups have, as in so many other ways, a special need to perform a difficult balancing act. The mentally handicapped are in special need of help in working out satisfactory adjustments to the "real" world.

CHAPTER 8

CIRCUMCISION

AFTER YEARS OF controversy, it is now generally agreed that circumcision (surgical removal of the foreskin covering the head or glans of the penis) is not justified on medical grounds. The alleged ill effects of not circumcising have been discounted both in terms of possible ill effects upon the male and upon his mate. Basic cleanliness under the foreskin is all that is needed to prevent accumulations of the normal secretion, smegma, which otherwise may harden under the foreskin just as fluid from the eyes, the so-called "sleep" hardens in the corners of the eyes in the morning. Such hardened accumulations may cause pain. The parent needs to assume responsibility for this basic cleanliness until such time as the child can learn to tend to himself.

In recent years, as parents have been confronted increasingly with the ritualistic nature of circumcision, more and more have elected not to have their infants circumcised. Consequently, uncircumcised little boys are now less likely to attract attention to themselves when showering or swimming with other boys. However, since the circumcised are still the majority in many communities, it is undoubtedly wise for parents to coach the uncircumcised with regard to the meaning of their difference so they will not be embarrassed, humiliated or angered by the comments or teasing of their circumcised fellows.

Question: Is circumcision never needed or desirable?

Answer: Of course it may be in individual cases, particularly to correct specific medical problems. For example, a foreskin may be too tight to permit emergence of the head or glans of the penis.

Question: What about members of special groups?

Answer: Here again the answer must be in terms of individual needs. In addition to the possible need to correct medical problems, it may be unrealistic to expect severely retarded individuals to tend to their own cleanliness, and circumcision may therefore become an important convenience. Clearly, too, individuals with inadequately functioning or missing hands or arms may be totally dependent upon others for this service. In such cases, circumcision might very well be the reasonable choice.

In conclusion. From a health standpoint, whether or not to circumcise is a decision best made on the basis of individual circumstances.

CHAPTER 9

MASTURBATION

W IDESPREAD CHANGE IN attitude toward masturbation is perhaps a major and irreversible feature of the modern sexual revolution. Masturbation has undoubtedly been one of the most common sexual practices during the course of human history. However, the general attitude toward this practice in our tradition has been that not only the behavior but the word itself has been taboo. The taboo did not prevent the behavior, but it did make the word virtually unusable—even though the behavior has been a matter of major concern in child rearing and among special groups in particular. Within the last few years, however, the word has become increasingly respectable and has even been headlined in popular newspapers where previously it could not even have been buried in the text of a news article.

Generally speaking, masturbation has reference to sexual self-stimulation directed toward climax or orgasm. In contrast, there is the common, private self-stimulation or fondling of the genitals by people generally and by infants, young children and members of various special groups. Such fondling is not ordinarily deliberately aimed at achieving climax even though, sometimes to the surprise of the particular individual, orgasm does occur.

Masturbation by males is known by all kinds of terms. These include "jerking off," "jacking off," "beating off," "beating one's meat," "whacking off" and so on. The masturbation taboo has applied most intensively to females and, even though widely practiced among them, has not acquired an extensive slang terminology. Having a female terminology, for it would of course imply that the behavior exists, which of course would be (or would until very recently have been) unthinkable to most. More respectably, masturbation has been termed "auto-eroticism," "self-abuse," "playing with oneself," "bad habit" and more derogatorily, "self-rape." With heavy religious overtones, it has been called "onanism" from the biblical (Genesis 38:9) account of Onan's "spilling his seed upon the ground" in defiance of Jehovah who proceeded to strike him dead. (The Onan story is now generally taken to mean that Onan committed *coitus interruptus* or withdrawal rather than father a child with his dead brother's wife as he was supposed to do. However, traditionally onanism has meant masturbation.) It may well be a healthy sign of the times that the secret male slang is less often heard, and in private conversation, the popular media and in social and educational settings people refer quite often and unabashedly to "masturbation."

Although masturbation is usually carried out by hand or by fingertips in the female, other means of stimulation are sometimes used. All manner of objects may be rubbed against the genitals or the genitals rubbed against them. For example, Kinsey found a few males capable of auto-fellatio or stimulation of one's own penis by one's own mouth; and in *Portnoy's Complaint*, Roth writes of using a cored apple. Female masturbation may range from rubbing the thighs together, using a gentle jet of warm water, employing a dildo or an electric vibrator. A few females may masturbate successfully by means of nipple stimulation and even by means of vivid sexual fantasies.

Masturbation is usually practiced in private but it may also occur in the company of another person or persons of the same or other sex. For example, a female's masturbating may be highly arousing to a male partner; in contrast, groups of boys have commonly made a game of group masturbation, the object being to see who could "come" first or farthest.

Since masturbation has reference to self-stimulation, "mutual masturbation" is misleading as a term for mutual stimulation by hand. Mutual stimulation by hand or "heavy petting" is more akin to mutual stimulation by mouth (69). For some, including many special group members, mutual hand stimulation is the preferred technique of intercourse because body positioning can be flexible and because hand pressure and movement can be so precisely adjusted to the desires of the couple. (In contrast, cunnilingus has reference to stimulation of the female genitals by male or female partners' mouth and tongue; and fellatio has reference to such stimulation of the penis by a partner.)

How commonly practiced is masturbation? Every indication is that no one should feel alone or even in a minority group for practicing it. As a matter of fact, this behavior is extremely common among both males and females, not only in childhood but during much of their lives. Indications are that at least seventy percent of females and ninety percent of males could be termed masturbators. Incidentally, this kind of derogatory terminology was formerly used moralistically and as a means of identifying the cause of individual and social decline. Almost no one bothers with such nonsense anymore; masturbation has increasingly come to be viewed as a natural and normal form of human sexual expression.

Most boys and girls discover masturbation around the time of puberty or shortly thereafter. Many little boys as well as girls discover orgasm long before puberty, even before their school years. Some adults are willing to point out that they do not remember a time in their lives when they did not know what an orgasm felt like. In contrast, some adults have never experienced the sensations of orgasm.

Sexual partners may or may not be available during the course of life, but masturbation tends to be available when release of sexual tension or simply gratification is desired. This is to say that during marriage and in the later years as well as in youth, masturbation is found by many to be, if not the only, at least the dependable outlet for sexual expression, regardless of availability or mood of a partner.

Question: Are you saying that masturbation is generally "good" rather than "bad" behavior during the course of life?

Answer: Definitely. Anti-masturbation people have yet to come up with evidence of clear and present danger associated with this behavior. On the other hand, leading students of human sexuality now argue that masturbation is not only normal and natural as well as legitimately pleasurable behavior, but also it may be very useful and beneficial. Among the young, it is certainly an aspect of self-understanding and a means whereby one's potential for experiencing and enjoying may be realized in a way that may be compared to visual or auditory pleasures. People who have experienced orgasm on their own do not have to be taught what they are looking for in sexual fulfillment with others. Marriage counselors and sex therapists now view masturbation as one of the important means whereby many people may learn to overcome sexual dysfunction (so-called "impotency" and "frigidity" in male and female respectively).

Husbands and wives have often unrealistically tended to be annoyed, feel cheated or otherwise upset upon learning of their mate's past or present masturbatory behavior. Thus it was somewhat unusual to hear a wife urge her husband to masturbate as often as possible. It seems that the man had just undergone a vasectomy. Since it is necessary for the male to ejaculate ten or so times after the operation before he can be confident that there are no residual sperm, for a time his sexual activity must be confined to masturbation or coition with the protection of contraception. Frequent masturbation for a few days seemed to her the efficient way of handling things.

Question: The traditional view of masturbation has been very ugly and has given rise to great fear and guilt feelings. If masturbation is harmless and even beneficial, why has it had such negative associations?

Answer: To begin with, it is important to realize that our evaluation of most things is culturally conditioned. Thus, in some societies outside of our tradition, masturbation is condemned and punished; in others it is accepted and even encouraged and in still others not much attention is paid to it one way or the other. In our own tradition, it has been very negatively viewed because of its condemnation by two of the most powerful influences in our society: religion and medicine. In our sacred literature, masturbation seems to be among the gravest of sins, punishable by death as are other forms of wastage of the male seed. This tradition has been enormously strong and influential for centuries and still profoundly influences behavior within families, in schools and in many churches.

In addition to this religious-moral condemnation has been the negative medical posture based in part on this tradition and also upon the observation that disturbed people tend to masturbate more or less openly. Medical observers jumped erroneously to the conclusion that the disturbance was caused by the masturbation—and also to the conclusion that the disturbance caused the masturbating. Books have been written on the subject of individual and social diseases, both physical and mental, alleged to be caused by masturbation; and less than two decades ago, psychiatric literature still teemed with examples of disorders attributed to masturbatory behavior. At one time or another virtually every known disease has been attributed to "excessive" masturbation. Finally, it took people like Anthony Comstock, author of our present postal obscenity laws, to put all this together: masturbation causes all manner of sickness, eventually death and since it is clearly against the will of God, damnation. With such an overlay of magic-minded verbiage and medical nonsense, is it any wonder that such negativism is at least perceived as groundless and is being outgrown? Not so many years ago it still seemed plausible for people to patent devices which would warn fathers by electrical signals that their sons in their beds needed to be saved from themselves. Today, however, it is probably safe to say that most clergymen dismiss masturbation as being not all that important, and most physicians do not view it as a psychiatric problem. Indeed, both groups in recent years have begun to express changed and generally positive views on the subject.

Question: What are the physical and mental effects of masturbation?

Answer: Today, medical and other experts generally agree that masturbation, no matter how frequently it is practiced, produces none of the harmful physical effects about which physicians warned in the past. Physiologically, sexual response in masturbation is the same as that in coitus; and neither has been shown to adversely affect physical performance. Anecdotal data of Pomeroy[1] and experimental research of my own[2] show no drop in athletic or measured physical output resulting from orgasmic release. In one case, a top runner broke a national record half an hour after he had masturbated to calm himself. However, other athletes avoid sexual release for some hours prior to competition, not for fear that it would weaken them but because of its possible relaxing effects, which they do not desire. There seems to be no evidence to support the claim that masturbation has adverse physical effects. On the contrary, Kinsey made the point that sexual arousal that does not result in orgasmic release is likely to distract people from their work, upset them and generally lower their efficiency.[3]

As to psychological effects, the same seems to be true. Few people take the old claims about masturbation causing "insanity," mental retardation, neurological damage or other symptoms seriously any more. Still, untold numbers of persons have suffered mental turmoil from childhood onward because of a sense of guilt about masturbation. It is probably fair to say that never have so many been so indebted to so little for so much anguish and guilt. Clearly, such upset is due not to the act of masturbation itself but to the entirely unnecessary feeling that one is bad, worthless, perverted or sick and therefore in need of punishment

[1] W. Pomeroy, Personal Communication (1970).

[2] W. R. Johnson, "Muscular Performance and Coitus," *J. of Sex Research*, Vol. 4 (August, 1968), pp. 247-248.

[3] A. Kinsey and others, *Sexual Behavior in the Human Male* (Philadelphia: W. B. Sanders, 1948).

or treatment for doing it. Thus, any adverse effects of masturbation are attributable not to the masturbation itself but to mistaken notions about it.

Quesion: Can masturbation be excessive?

Answer: Of course it can—in the same sense that such things as eating, reading or watching television can be excessive. None of these things is in itself bad or harmful. But they may suggest the presence of a problem. Thus, if an individual is watching television "too much" because there are few other satisfactions available in life, then the problem is obviously not his addiction to television but the paucity of other satisfactions. TV is not the culprit; it is the lack of a challenging environment.

Excessive masturbation by children has sometimes been found to be due to skin irritation, poorly fitting clothing or to an adjustment problem. When one mother complained that her ten-year-old son would do little else in his free time but masturbate, questioning revealed that because the boy had failed to learn basic play or sport skills he was constantly teased and ridiculed when he attempted to play with other children. He had also failed to acquire appropriate social skills learned in play, with the result that the range of sources of satisfaction in his life was greatly restricted. Individual work with a clinical physical educator soon led to acquisition of the needed play and sport skills and paved the way for successful play and other interaction with his peers. Clearly, his excessive masturbation had been the symptom of a problem rather than the problem itself.

In another case, a mildly retarded boy made a practice of roughly shaking, slapping and otherwise abusing his penis until it would become erect and bruised. He pretended to greatly enjoy this activity when with the gang. But actually, he had originally chanced to discover that his peculiar behavior attracted a great deal of wondering attention. Since this was virtually the only attention that he got, he had capitalized on this one claim to social recognition. Helping him was not a matter of attacking this particular symptom, but of helping him to acquire physical and social skills to gain group acceptance without having to resort to such extreme self-damaging measures.

It is well to emphasize that the term "excessive" is vague and undefined and may in actuality reflect the greater or lesser sexual drive of one person versus another. There is, indeed, wide individual variation in sex drive and capacity to engage in sexual activity. St. Paul was grateful that he was not diverted from his divine mission by a sex drive. Some people are rarely if ever "troubled" by sexual arousals, and some are not able to achieve satisfying relief no matter how they try. At the other extreme, there are individuals who are chronically troubled by their sex drive and perhaps get themselves into some degree of trouble trying to find ways to satisfy it. Some males may masturbate several times a day, and some females may experience even more orgasmic responses than males if they discover their capacity for multiple orgasms during single stimulation periods. Still, there are always physiological limits. Clearly, people on a scale between extremes of responsiveness would likely have very different notions of what constitutes "excessive" masturbation.

Some men masturbate in advance of lovemaking so as to check their excitement, thereby helping avoid too quick ejaculation with their partners. This is quite different from masturbating in lieu of engaging in sex with an available partner. In the latter case, masturbation may be excessive in the sense that it may reflect "copping out" based on fear of failure or fear of the other sex.

Question: Why do people have fantasies during masturbation and what is their significance?

Answer: In the first place, some people report they do not have fantasies while masturbating. They say they know exactly what to do to bring on the desired sensations, simply enjoy the build-up of their feelings and have no need to enhance arousal by fantasy. Others, probably the majority, help themselves to focus attention on sex and enhance their arousal by imagining as vividly as possible those things which tend to be highly associated with sexual excitement. For this reason some people define pornography as material that is looked at with one hand—which is to say while masturbating; the individual reads or looks at pictures which excite his imagination and help him or her masturbate successfully.

The problem with masturbatory fantasy is that it is likely to further intensify guilt and anxiety feelings being generated by the masturbating itself. So the individual needlessly ends up feeling still more contemptuous of himself, still more guilty, still more doubtful of "normality" with special reference to mental health or sanity. True, people are sometimes amazed if not appalled by things and activities which may fire their imaginations during masturbation or coition for that matter. After all, they may wonder, what kind of person am I to have such imaginings as sexual contact with animals, with being raped or otherwise being forced into sex, with perhaps even heightening arousal by fantasies of violence? Some people who finally get over their guilt feelings for masturbating simply switch to similar feelings about their fantasies.

If, instead of thinking that they are indulging in fantasied perversion or getting dreadful insights into their own secret thoughts, people were to view their masturbatory and other fantasies as their own private artwork which, for reasons of their own, focus and heighten sexual feeling, they could make use of their fantasies and not abuse them. In spite of the dreadful things that people, including many counselors, have said about both masturbation and masturbatory fantasies, there seems to be no actual evidence of harmful effect of either. And both have been major bulwarks in the course of human history against the frustrations of unavailable social and sexual activity of one's heart's desire.

Question: Does masturbation reduce sexual competency or gratification with a mate?

Answer: No. This question should be recognized for what it really is, namely a last-ditch stand against masturbatory release or gratification. Girls especially have been led to believe that, "Okay, you can get away with this now but it will destroy you as a future sexual partner." Bunk! Generally speaking, as the Kinsey findings clearly indicated, females who have not experienced orgasm prior to coition have tended to take longer to become good sexual partners than those who already had some knowledge of sexual satisfaction and how to achieve it.

One girl wrote: "I was profoundly uneasy about masturbation and a nurse's punishment of my masturbatory bathing activity. Later I was sure that I was one of those who masturbated excessively and that this was symptomatic of nymphomania if nothing else. I was sure that it would interfere with successful marital adjustment, and my husband should never know. Hence it took three years and much new sex education to even get up the nerve and self-belief to tell him how I did it so that I could teach him for gratifying foreplay. To tell him before would imply that I did actually masturbate, ugly creature. Finally, it took months of sexual activity with my husband and sex education before I could tolerate his manipulation of my genitals without all the massive resistance and shame and denial that this was just masturbating, repeating that awful thing I did. The guilt carried over to totally block heterosexual release."

Was all this difficulty caused by the masturbation or by the dreadful, traditional attitudes toward it? When she changed her attitude, masturbation became useful rather than evil and destructive.

These days young men and women who have been exposed to reasonably good sex education take it for granted that their mates very probably masturbated while growing up and are likely to continue doing so from time to time in the best of marriages. Still, however, marriage counseling is still sometimes needed to help couples realize that such behavior is not somehow "bad," cheating on the mate or a perversion.

It would be a mistake to assume from the foregoing that masturbation is necessarily a healthy behavior. As pointed out earlier, it may represent compensatory behavior and signal the need for help. In marriage, too, it may signal a problem requiring careful evaluation for its meaning, perhaps pathological meaning. For example, in a seminar for interdenominational clergymen, a participant insisted it was masturbation which had brought about divorce among one of his perfectly normal congregation couples. When pressed, he pointed out that the husband would masturbate on the wife while they were in bed. The wife didn't like it; ergo, it must have been masturbation which destroyed the marriage. At the time of the seminar, there was no opportunity to seek out the full meaning of this unspoken message; but message it surely was. Professional help would doubtless have identified some specific communication breakdown, peculiar sex attitudes or hostilities. At the very least, the hopefully good name of masturbation would not have been sullied yet again by a confusion of causes and symptoms.

Question: How common is it for people to have difficulty in their efforts to masturbate?

Answer: Many males and females experience periods in their lives when masturbation to orgasm is extremely easy, with orgasmic release achieved with very little stimulation or even by accident. Writers often give a misimpression when they discuss masturbation as though it were something people can do successfully at any time they wish.

Difficulty in achieving orgasmic release may be due to a variety of reasons ranging from overwhelming guilt feelings to excessive fatigue, intoxication or inability to concentrate on sexual thoughts and fantasies. Sometimes people simply fail to utilize a satisfactory lubricant and thereby create discomfort from friction. Occasionally medical problems requiring minor surgery or even treatment for an allergy may block orgasmic release.

In many cases, individuals need only experiment with various methods in order to achieve success. (We are rarely always successful at anything.) For example, one girl who had been experiencing difficulty found that a small jet of warm water directed at the clitoris proved entirely satisfactory for achieving multiple orgasms without the need for other excitatory aids. Others have found an electrical vibrator directed mainly upon and around the clitoris most useful. Men have been helped by using satisfactory lubricating material (baby oil, cold cream). Both males and females tend to be helped by finding a comfortable position, learning to concentrate on what they are doing and perhaps making use of what are for them erotic aids in the form of pictures or writings.

Sex counselors often help individuals who are having more serious response problems by introducing them to a gradual training sequence, perhaps designated "homework," somewhat as follows: Caress the sensitive bodily parts to cultivate and enjoy pleasurable sensations. Gently caress and stroke the genitals, especially the penis or inner labia and clitoris, cultivating pleasurable sensations and some arousal with no effort being made to reach climax—merely to find, enjoy and build up sensation. Gradually, with whatever aids may be useful (even hypnosis in some cases), focus is placed upon the heightening of sensation which usually with practice culminates in orgasmic release.

As people lack privacy, grow older and/or have been subjected to anti-sexual training, their masturbatory efforts may meet with more or less frustration. However, this is no calamity; it does not mean that the individual is "washed up," "no good" or inadequate. Time and further effort are very likely to produce success.

In conclusion. Students of human sexuality and of mental health are increasingly taking the position that masturbation may

be regarded as part of the normal process of development, including sexual maturation, and as a legitimate human behavior at
all ages. Lacking health if not societal and legal reasons for
combating masturbation, teachers and counselors might best
relax themselves about the whole matter and merely attempt to
help the individual live successfully with the existing biological,
psychological and sociological realities. It is perhaps a major
tribute to the human life force that the most extreme and per-
sistent efforts to eliminate masturbatory behavior—ranging all the
way from severe punishment, including death, to sterilization
and to special chastity belts—have generally failed. Now that
the most diligent effort has failed to produce any evidence of
clear and present danger associated with masturbation, a new
look at the whole subject seems entirely in order. There seems
to be a growing consensus that no one, neither child nor adult,
should be subjected to indignities, let alone persecution, for
sharing a near universal interest which might, under certain
circumstances at least, be encouraged rather than discouraged.
Traditional direct or indirect preventive actions have made little
or no sense because they have presumed the culpability of the
behavior itself. On the other hand, it makes a great deal of sense
to help change attitudes toward this behavior, while at the same
time helping those in need of social perspective to adjust themselves successfully to the demands of the real world.

SEX PLAY WITH OTHER AND OWN SEX

T HE HUMAN BODY is interesting to people; and in spite of training to the contrary, children look at and touch each other's bodies
when the opportunity arises. In due course, genital play is to be
expected among members of like and unlike sexes. Where nudity
is permitted, the penis is likely to attract special attention, partly
because of its novelty to little girls and also because of its
interesting changeability, being sometimes small and soft and
at other times much larger and erect. The scrotum moves about
in interesting ways, especially in response to temperature change.
The more children are confined to the company of their own sex,
like adults, the more likely they are to take an interest in sex
play with members of their own sex.

Sex play may be direct and in the form of manual stimulation
and manipulation. It may evolve into mouth stimulation. It may
include lying on top of one another in coition-type positions.
Or, in the case of children, it may be "playing doctor," which
tends to give it an air of legitimacy. Playing doctor is a good
cover-up. Other common forms of play may include urination
for distance contests (girls can get very good at this), penis
length in hard and soft state contests and less often, speed of
ejaculation contests. The most unusual I have heard of was the
old Swiss contest to see who could carry a bucket of water
farthest on an erect penis. Girls in a well-known Pennsylvania
finishing school had a little contest to determine how many
couples could reach climax before a particular record ended.
Rarely do parents recount such playful episodes of their child-

hood and youth to their own children—particularly when they find their own children so engaged.

I have never known any such behavior, though it might include children who are blood relatives, to have damaging effects prior to puberty when intercourse may (but usually will not) give rise to unwanted pregnancy. Of course, if participants in such games brood about it and tell themselves over and over that they are dirty, useless rats for doing such things, they may upset themselves. But it is the brooding, not the play, that upsets them. After all, if tennis were forbidden but some people played it anyway, a certain percentage would likely brood and denounce themselves over that, too.

Sex play behavior is entirely natural if one may judge by its occurrence in animals and its universal appearance among human young. Still, these experiences are likely to be major and perhaps traumatic episodes in which the child is confronted with the conflict between his biology and the morality of his society. And such experiences enhance personal conflict because the play is likely to be uniquely gratifying and thereby self-perpetuating; at the same time, however, adult reactions are likely to be so vehement and perhaps violent that the child may feel badly about himself generally. He may even resent and fear sexual feelings generally because giving in to them risks the threat not only of punishment but of loss of love from parents or other esteemed adults. These circumstances often give rise to the apparently paradoxical situation in which the very child who initiates the sex play attempts to rescue his self-esteem and esteem of his parents by tattling on friends. The informer may win adult approval, but there is the backlash of peer anger and resentment to be dealt with.

One of the common responses of young people to the parental upset over sex play is for sexual interest to go underground. That is, the reasonably intelligent child soon learns what will get him into trouble with adults. And since he or she does not wish to abandon the fun, ways of avoiding adult notice are soon discovered. Adults may get the impression that youngsters lose their interest in sex at about this time (and think happily of their having entered the period of "latency"). But childhood sexual interest has merely gone underground and continues to flourish if the opportunity arises.

Question: Isn't childhood sex play ever harmful?

Answer: Of course, like virtually everything else, it can under certain circumstances be harmful. For example, if children poke sharp or breakable objects into their own or each others' bodies, physical harm may be done. Psychological harm may also result from the explosive, angry behavior of adults or older children. For example, I know a man who has really suffered for nearly half a century because of a sexual play episode which occurred with another boy when he was eight years old. It seems that the two were engaged in manual and some oral penis play when they were come upon by his father. Father was outraged and beat his son but, more devastatingly, used words which planted profound doubts in the boy's mind as to his normality and the lingering fear that he was and is basically homosexual. The question is, what gave rise to the years of doubt and even of anguish? The sex play itself—or the father's reaction to it?

Fortunately, most young people probably do not take their parents' reactions so seriously and, as I have indicated, merely take the whole business underground where parents remain for the most part blissfully unaware of it. For example, as the famous woman writer Rey Anthony pointed out, when at age three her mother caught her peeing with a little boy in her doll house, she beat her, threatened to knock her head off and promised even more dire punishment if she ever caught her doing that kind of thing again. Rey simply remarked "She never did," which is to say that Rey was wise enough to outmaneuver her mother after that and never again be caught. In brief, unlike the boy who was terribly vulnerable to his father's opinion and threats, Rey was bothered neither by her mother's blows and yanking by the arm nor by her mother's angry outcry. She merely learned her lesson about the adult world and went about her business. Incidentally, she did find it incongruous that her minister grandfather would pay her a nickel to let him "play" with her nonexistent breasts and her "pussy."

Question: Does like-sex play give rise to homosexuality?

Answer: Homosexuality is a black label. Just how does one qualify to be placed under this label? If one is labelled homosexual for any homosexual act, then of course sex play to orgasm is homosexuality. If continued, such sex play is likely eventually to give rise to orgasmic release.

On the other hand, what is usually meant by this question is: Does homosexual sex play in childhood give rise to preference for exclusive or fixated homosexuality in adulthood? The answer is definitely no. Sleuths of homosexual etiology do not take such play seriously as a "cause" of homosexuality. Prison inmates of both sexes and other such sexually segregated groups sometimes recall having had homosexual gratification in childhood and may in their frustration seek out such gratification as the only kind available to them under the circumstances. However, when circumstances allow they revert to their preferred heterosexual orientation.

Question: Would you encourage or at least ignore homosexual sex play?

Answer: The entire approach in this volume is to present information as accurate as possible about behavior and then to leave it to the reader to make application with respect to specific individuals and circumstances. It would be absurd to further stigmatize a handicapped child with the dread label "homosexual." On the other hand, similar children or adults confined in sexually segregated institutions for many years have brightened their lives with homosexual activity.

Question: Is sex play confined primarily to children?

Answer: Of course not. It occurs or is likely to occur at any age and may be initiated by members of either sex. In recent years, some marriage manuals have even been bestowing a considerable respectability upon the sex play of lovers, newlyweds and sex partners generally. This is undoubtedly a healthy development. If observed and reported, much of this behavior is against the law, particularly if mouth-genital contact is involved, and may be severely punished by the authorities.

Question: Are there matters of special concern with respect to sex play among special group members?

Answer: Of course. No matter how liberal society seems to become in sexual attitude, children and probably most special members are generally bound by fundamentalist views of sex. The prevailing societal view holds sexuality at best inappropriate among children and older people. It does not cross anyone's mind that a blind, crippled, palsied or convalescing individual may be climbing the walls with sexual desire. Frequently they are, but as far as "society" is concerned, this is unthinkable.

As is often the case, special group members, their parents and others who work with them are often walking a tightrope where they are attempting to express a near-universal and generally harmless human desire while at the same time making the necessary concessions to social attitudes.

In conclusion. Body play involving stroking and caressing is likely to lead to sex play—which can be a thrilling and safe diversion. Mates are now encouraged to engage in such activity as a form of affectionate communication and build-up to coition. However, it is usually seen as something intrinsically "bad" for children, and out of place at best among special group members (as in the case of masturbation, sex play may be viewed as a manifestation or symptom of a physical or mental handicap).

Except as special group members are able to create living situations for themselves, it seems unlikely that sex play will ever be an accepted form of recreation for special group members.

CHAPTER 11

MENSTRUATION

Generally speaking, each month from puberty (around thirteen years of age) to menopause (around fifty), the walls of the uterus gradually build up a layer of tissue and blood, and, if pregnancy does not occur, this is discharged within four or five days as the menstrual flow. On the average, about fourteen days before the beginning of the *next* menstrual period, the ovaries expel an ovum (ovulation) which soon enters the oviduct or Fallopian tube. If sperm are in the oviducts or even the uterus when ova are in these regions, pregnancy is likely to occur. Some women with very regular cycles can predict when they will ovulate by counting backward about fourteen days from their next expected beginning of menstruation. A few women even have a recognizable sensation or other symptom when they ovulate and can therefore tell quite accurately those days when conception is possible for them. Unfortunately, the majority of women cannot tell when ovulation is or will be taking place. This uncertainty as to when sexual intercourse is likely to result in pregnancy means that there is no predictable "safe" period for them.

Individual differences are illustrated by the fact that even though, on the average, girls begin to menstruate by about thirteen, some begin when they are in the fourth grade (nine or ten years old) and others do not begin until they are in college (seventeen or eighteen years old). Their starting time, menarche, may be perfectly normal for them, although medical confirmation should certainly be sought. Also, both early and late menstruation may very well pose problems for menstrual education. When should little girls be told about menstruating, the menstrual flow and what to do about it if they are not to be victims of the shock of suddenly starting, without preparation, perhaps in school?

Obviously, it is better to be too early than too late with education along these lines; and so the tendency has been to try to provide menstrual education by the time most girls have reached the age of ten.

Question: How can girls be helped to adjust to menstruating?

Answer: Mothers and older sisters, in particular, can help young girls to realize that this is a normal and natural behavior of females by making no great secret of it and letting the younger girl observe how they deal with it. If mothers in particular can help to convey a natural acceptance of this function and its implications, the girl will have a useful model to follow. Thoughtful mothers and teachers realize that a small percentage of girls will begin menstruating exceptionally early, and they therefore make known to all of the girls that this can happen and what to do about it—namely where to go for guidance, a sanitary napkin and so on.

Among many peoples ,including those in our own tradition, the menstrual flow has had a special stigma attached to it. It is unclean, the "curse." If little girls can be taught to view menstrual blood the same as any other blood, with no special evil or derogatory meaning, the girl is less likely to find menstruation a traumatic, depressing experience.

Question: What restrictions should be placed upon physical activity during menstruation?

Answer: There are exceptions, but as a general rule, girls and women can continue to engage in those activities that they are used to but should probably attempt to avoid new activities which require particular physiological adjustment. Thus, for example, girls accustomed to strenuous swimming in chilly water can oftentimes continue this activity even though menstruating. However, a girl who is unaccustomed to such activity might very well experience more or less severe cramping if she attempts it while menstruating. I have occasionally encountered mothers in our clinic who routinely put their young daughters to bed for three or four days every time they menstruated. Of course this is unnecessary and undesirable cautiousness, but it should be borne in mind that girls and parents of girls in special groups are oftentimes deprived of reasonable sex education including menstrual education. Therefore they are left on their own to surmise what is best to do. Experience in other situations has often taught them that they need to be especially cautious, and so caution tends to be the watchword in this regard also.

Question: How are females affected psychologically by menstruation, and why?

Answer: Here again individual differences are marked. Some girls report not feeling any differently at all at this time. Others feel about as usual but they may seem unusually critical or irritable to others. And still others find themselves unmistakably irritable, depressed or "bitchy." "I can't even stand myself sometimes at that time of the month," some say.

There is considerable evidence that "menstrual blues" are due not so much to hormonal changes as to negative traditional training, Protestant girls tending to have less emotional upheaval than the more traditionally indoctrinated Jewish or Catholic girls.[1]

Still, hormones are very powerful chemicals which can affect behavior. It stands to reason that the very negative traditional attitudes toward "the curse" are likely to affect individual females' responses. However, many physicians are convinced that some women with a generally relaxed feeling towards menstruation acquire physical symptoms treatable by medication. For example, some women evi-

---

[1] K. E. Paige, "Women Learn to Sing the Menstrual Blues," *Psychology Today*, Vol. 7 (September, 1973), p. 41.

dently become very irritable, because of a fluid build-up in the brain (edema) or other hormonal change; this condition can be relieved promptly by medication which reduces the pressure. In brief, it is undoubtedly true that menstrual problems of psychological nature may be minimized by depicting this function to girls in a positive light. However, a physiological basis for psychological distress cannot be ignored, particularly in those cases in which menstruation and menstrual flow have not been presented to the child in grim or otherwise negative terms.

Question: Are there special considerations with regard to the menstruating of girls and women in special groups?

Answer: Yes, there may well be a number of special considerations. In the first place, parents, teachers and others responsible for such girls need to expect less in the way of help with menstrual education and counseling than is available for other girls via schools and various girls' organization. For example, schools and girls' groups commonly make decisions, presumably with the help of qualified experts, as to when menstrual education might best begin. Moreover, they usually develop curriculum guides, assemble materials, determine learning goals with regard to both attitudes and factual information and propose learning experiences whereby such goals may be achieved. On the other hand, girls whose special status deprives them of such programs are dependent on whatever knowledge and ingenuity their mothers and others working with them can or are willing to muster. Boys in special groups are frequently deprived of any serious introduction to menstruation or its meaning.

It is sometimes hard for parents of special children to realize that whatever developmental problem they may have, they may mature normally or even early in terms of reproductory functions. Unevenness of physical, emotional, social and intellectual development is to be expected of all children and menstruation at the usual age by special girls had best be anticipated. Caution warns that a certain number of them will begin to menstruate well before age thirteen; and a certain number will begin considerably later. Not beginning by thirteen probably does not mean a medical problem, but it may.

To the extent that the special group girl is slower to grasp concepts or is more vulnerable to upset over being "different," special adjustments need to be made in terms of emphasizing naturalness, universality, basic know-now and simplicity. Long explanations and big words can be frightening in themselves. Of course a child's mother or surrogate mother can play the crucial role by using her own menstrual experience as a model for understanding something of the phenomenon and how to deal with it. I have found that some mothers are revolted at the idea of letting their daughters observe such intimate matters. On the other hand, many others who also prefer privacy are willing to sacrifice it to a degree in the interests of helping their daughters make an easier, more natural adjustment to it.

Generally speaking, if a natural setting can be established with regard to menstruation, girls will learn about it as they learn other things. That is, the less bright will need more in the way of repetition, demonstrations and practice; the brighter will need less.

In conclusion. In recent years, women have been growing increasingly tired of having a natural function represented as a badge of shame or evidence of psychological inferiority. As communication on the subject continues to improve and women refuse to pass on the old attitudes, a healthy adjustment to menstruation will gradually emerge. Girls and women in special groups have every right to benefit from this development.

CHAPTER 12

NOCTURNAL EMISSIONS (WET DREAMS)

UNLIKE GIRLS, BOYS do not do anything commercially valuable like menstruating at puberty. They have therefore tended to be deprived of even the basic reproduction education that the companies selling sanitary protection products have helped make respectable for girls. Among other things, boys have tended to be deprived of information and guidance concerning an equally natural phenomenon, nocturnal emissions or wet dreams which because of ignorance can give rise to extreme anxiety.

At puberty the male genitals, like those of the female, tend to become larger and very sensitive. At this time, the boy begins to ejaculate at orgasm. At puberty and in the early teens, very little stimulation of the frequently erect penis may be sufficient to bring about ejaculation. Similarly, with or without accompanying erotic dreams, ejaculation may occur during sleep. If the boy has been led to realize that such nocturnal emissions are a normal part of growing up as a male, he is likely to enjoy the experience rather than be upset by it. On the other hand, if he has been brought up to fear and perhaps dread his sexual responses, and if he faces this development armed only with ignorance, he is likely to view his wet dreams as evidence that something is wrong. If he has been trained to have a negative attitude toward his sexuality, the new development is likely to give rise to strong guilt feelings and he is sure to think badly of himself. After all, it probably means that he is masturbating too much or something has gone wrong with him. His wet sheets will be discovered along with his guilt and shame.

106

It is for reasons such as these that many men describe their nocturnal emissions as having caused some of the most anguished experiences of their early lives. Of course this is a little like feeling guilty over having one's blood pressure change in response to exercise or emotional arousal or having the pupils of one's eyes change in response to light changes. But such is the traditional attitude toward many normal sexual responses.

A great many young (and sometimes not so young) males in special groups experience wet dreams just as other males do.

Question: Are wet dreams always preceded or accompanied by erotic dreams?

Answer: Some writers have claimed this is so, pointing out that even though the individual does not remember the dream upon awakening, he very likely was dreaming about sex and thereby precipitated the emission. On the other hand, it is possible to argue that just as emission by masturbation need not necessarily be associated with sexy thoughts or fantasies, high sexual energy during a sleep may require no supplemental psychological boost.

Question: Are there special implications associated with nocturnal emissions for members of special groups?

Answer: There need not be. But they are often viewed as still another "problem." The point is that these are spontaneous sleeptime experiences which need not be associated with guilt or other negative emotions. Indeed, they may very well be viewed as positive aspects of maturation and sexuality.

Males sometimes report having awakened enough to succeed in actually reaching orgasm by hand stimulation— and thereby they feel that they have done a bad thing by willfully masturbating. The more positive view is that if the wet dream needs a little help in reaching climax, there is no good reason why it should not get it.

Question: Do females experience anything similar to nocturnal emissions?

Answer: Yes, except of course they do not ejaculate. On the other hand, they do experience high sexual arousal during sleep which may include reaching orgasm as well as producing a considerable moistening of internal and external sexual structures. Many females report a quite lively sleeptime sex life which, even though commonly associated with strong guilt feelings, at least has the virtue of not producing telltale evidence of semen as it does in males. The girl can tell herself that she didn't do it on purpose and avoid having to blame herself. Incidentally, during the Middle Ages, it was believed that a diabolical creature, the *incubus*, ravished girls in their sleep, just as a *succubus* imposed similar sexual gratification upon males. Thus magic-mindedness rescued the individual from personal responsibility while at the same time it reinforced the prevading anti-sexual theology of the time.

In conclusion. Wet dreams are a part of the normal maturation process. They are a problem only if viewed as a problem. A generally naturalistic, positive view of sexuality in the maturing male can assure that these potentially enjoyable experiences will not become traumatic. Any of the bodily changes of puberty, including pubic hair and deepening of voice, may give rise to concern. However, the maturation process can be explained simply to children at appropriate times and in appropriate ways. Sexual developments, including wet dreams, can merely be included in what is explained about growing up.

CHAPTER 13

"DIRTY" WORDS

ONE OF THE major means of attempting to make sex education and counseling respectable is to take great care to use "correct" language. The "correct" language of sex is medical, which is for the most part Latin. Latin is a dead language, and it is perhaps reflective of our traditional rejectionist attitude toward sex that its proper language has been considered Latin. However, the once respectable "four-letter" English words are still very much alive and understood by everyone. Children learn them at a very early age—from parents, siblings and neighbors. Because of the very special way in which they are used, children then use them, learn that they must not use them and then learn to use them, written and and spoken, when they can. This pattern persists throughout life.

"Vulgar language" means "language of the people." The "people" use it whether or not they are supposed to, but selectively on a time and place basis. For example, fathers (and mothers these days) who cuss on the job to a great extent, may be most punitive toward their own children for violation of dirty-word taboos at home. The taboo against dirty words used in the wrong circumstances is unbelievably strong, often much stronger than any taboo against the actual behavior to which the words refers. For example, a Hollywood or T.V. starlet would probably disappoint people if she did not have occasional sexual affairs, but if she is caught by reporters using vulgar language her reputation is likely to suffer.

In recent years, there has been considerable relaxation of the dirty-word taboo in popular entertainment as well as on college campuses. Some authors have gone so far as to urge the free use of "cuss" words as a harmless way of letting off steam and sometimes communicating feelings harmlessly but effectively. They also argue that since words are nothing but words, it is foolish and even dangerous to invest them with the power to upset and anger. Still, the fact remains that dirty words used at the "wrong" time can get people, including those in special groups, into very real trouble.

Question: What should be done about the use of dirty words by children?

Answer: In the first place, this is not really a very important matter. Children swear because they quickly note a certain emphasis or emotionality in the swearing of their parents, other adults and other children. They repeat these words, and frequently are rewarded with laughter or an unusual amount of attention. Presently they express emotion with the words just as they have heard others do. Eventually they are punished for this and usually these words go underground. Soon they become a major factor in the language of a peer group and very possibly a means of secretly expressing resentment or rebellion against the "ruling class." This use of language continues into adulthood when they frequently talk very differently in their club and sport activities than when they are around their families. Similarly, women have tended to talk quite differently when in the dorm or other all-female situations than when they are with mixed groups.

There is unquestionably a caste system when it comes to use of forbidden language, and children are definitely in the lower class. They soon learn from experience that careful distinctions need to be made with regard to time or place and cussing or more serious consequences must be dealt with.

Two considerations are especially important. First, why is the child using words which he knows will probably bring trouble down on his head? His feelings must be very strong to virtually invite punishment. Secondly, why are the adults so concerned? Why are they so "uptight" about words? There was the case of a school which was about to expel a boy for having sworn when told that he had to take an extra lap around the playground for being slow to get in line. However, discussion with the teachers and principal revealed that the boy's offense was really not all that grave and that perhaps the basic question was why were they reacting so violently?

Question: With regard to sex and elimination, why do people go on using obscene or vulgar language when there are perfectly acceptable words available?

Answer: Vulgar language is considered obscene, which is to say unuseable. But it should be remembered that vulgar language is the "language of the people" and the old English words tend to come more easily for more people than the Latin medical equivalents. There is also the enjoyment of getting away with violating a taboo.

Another reason for using forbidden words is that often these are the only words that particular individuals know and to them they are perfectly legitimate. For example, a child from the country or ghetto may simply not know what the teacher is talking about when she gives instructions about what to do when one must urinate; this may be true too of the patient who is given instruction by the public health nurse in proper language about the genitals or elimination.

Serious teachers and medical personnel often realize that they have to overcome their own irrational attitudes toward language if they are to serve their pupils or patients. Children do not benefit from punishment for using dirty words. But they may benefit from learning that one set of words is perfectly okay at home or in the neighborhood but another set must be learned if one is to get along in school or hold a job. Similarly, if school and medical people are serious about wanting to do their jobs, they will overcome their own over-reactions against what may well be the only language the pupil or patient knows so as to communicate effectively and get the job done.

Question: What if you realize that "Sticks and stones may break your bones but names will never hurt you"—but you go on being upset by "dirty" words and can't use or discuss them even when you want to?

Answer: People *learn* to react that way and can learn to react in other ways. The important first step, but only the first step, is the realization that words are only words and we don't have to react to them in extreme ways. Then comes the matter of adding feelings and behavior to understanding. Try having someone say the objectionable word(s) to you over and over until finally they bore rather than upset you. Starting at a whisper, then building up, try saying the words over and over again to yourself. Work in front of a mirror. Tape record and then play back. Clown with the word, say it angrily, playfully, teasingly. Presently you will say "piss" as easily as you say "miss," "fuck" as "luck" or "duck."

But don't forget! Most of the rest of the world is not deconditioned to such words. You're operating in two worlds; and sometimes it's most important to keep in mind which you're in at any particular time.

Question: What about dirty words and drawings on walls, blackboards?

Answer: In the first place, the best way to discourage the behavior is to ignore it. If a commotion is made, it may very well be getting the desired results: the authorities are being bugged. For another possibility, some people have obtained what they considered good results by setting aside a wall or other area in the lavatory for just such expression by pupils or inmates. Certainly blackboards invite being written on; and who can resist being a little shocking now and again?

However, when such writings and drawings are particularly numerous or emotional, questions as to their possible special meaning may be raised. Are they an attempt to convey a message that should be heard and acted upon? Is this felt to be the only means of communication open to an individual or group? In other words, the writings may well signal a problem needing attention.

When tempted to be outraged by the writings and 'artwork" of pupils, residents and inmates, it is well to bear in mind that those particular individuals did not invent the idea of such expression. Some of the most ancient drawings of man on his cave walls were erotic in nature—about as primitive as much produced today. Virtually all great artists have produced erotic art, often a great deal of it. And many of our most popular heroes from Benjamin Franklin to Mark Twain have taken great pleasure in their "dirty" writings. Words are "awful" only if we so define them.

Question: What about the use of dirty words by special group members?

Answer: Virtually everything said above applies equally to special group members. Generally speaking, special group members are perfectly aware of how to play the word game and when they can get away with what. It is true that some special group members may need help in learning matters of time and place with regard to word usage. However, it is easy to overdo efforts to normalize individuals so that they can "get along." Cleanliness, neatness, orderliness and no bad words may help keep you out of trouble and make life more manageable. Still, overconcern with such matters can also put a damper on the individual's spontaneity. We have seen overly clean and neat children benefit greatly from learning to relax, play, get dirty and disheveled. And what a breakthrough it may be to be able to cuss when hurt or angry. Regrettably, perhaps, this is a cursing society; and acquiring the ability to cuss appropriately may well signal an improved ability to be in on the ways of the society.

Still, what may be considered good, healthy cussing or "normal" wall writing on the part of most people may mean trouble to the special group member. Here again is the old tightrope walking act: how to provide the usual outlets and gratifications, while at the same time avoiding or controlling behaviors which further complicate life. It can usually be managed. But at any rate, let's avoid giving the impression that they are evil, rat-like creatures for doing what everyone else has probably done—or wanted to.

In conclusion. Our society does not tend to be rational about such things as dirty words, and therefore special group members may need to try especially hard to work out a reasonable adjustment to this ambiguous situation. Concerned parents, teachers, counselors and others may need to help the individual avoid self-defeating behavior while at the same time not adding an impossible adjustment problem of conformity to a different situation. For example, I was recently conducting a program on sex education and counseling of the handicapped in a large hotel room. While showing films on sexual enjoyment possibilities for handicapped people, I stepped out and passed another large room in the hotel where the National Rifle Association was showing a film on hunting and the efficient killing of small animals. I was struck by the fact that the two audiences were very sympathetically involved in their own films; but had the films been reversed, sex education films being shown to the riflemen and the hunting film being shown to the people concerned with special groups, each would have considered the other group's film exceedingly obscene and objectionable, both in terms of content and language.

Our pluralistic society requires that somehow people adjust to a world in which such extreme differences in standards concerning word usage do exist.

CHAPTER 14

HOMOSEXUALITY

H OMOSEXUALITY REFERS TO sexual activity between or among members of the same sex. Female homosexuals are often referred to as lesbians because of the fame brought to the island of Lesbos where the ancient Greek poetess Sappho set up a school for women and wrote poetry of her love for women.

In our Judeo-Christian tradition, homosexuality has been considered one of the graver sins, punishable by death. As with other ancient religious taboos, when Christianity emerged the taboo became the basis not only of religious but also of moral and legal proscriptions. Even today to a great many people, male homosexuality is against God and immoral. It continues to be against the law in most states (generally as implied by sodomy laws against oral and anal sex). Now that there is less widespread belief in the religious concept of sin, condemnation of male homosexuality is much more commonly based upon the psychiatric concept of psychological sickness. It is often viewed as a personality disorder comparable to neurotic or psychotic states requiring intensive treatment. However, in very recent years both homosexual and heterosexual spokesmen for the homosexual community have been arguing that generally (outside of prison and other forced sex-segregated situations) homosexuality is merely a legitimate sexual preference, at least part of the time, of a minority group in society. In 1974, a majority of the membership of the American Psychiatric Association voted in favor of this view. That is, it removed homosexuality from its official listing of mental disorders. Overnight, numerous people were *defined* out of mental illness.

Interestingly, female homosexuality has never been taken very seriously. This difference in attitude is probably based upon the male-dominated society's belief that what women do doesn't matter much and upon the fact that women have no seed to waste as men do. The women provided a kind of garden in which the male's precious seed might grow, and it was the seed that was to be wasted. The carryover of this more lenient attitude is seen in the fact that even though female homosexuality is exceedingly common in modern times, it never attracts the publicity that male homosexuality does. Moreover, during a ten-year period in New York studied by Kinsey, there were tens of thousands of arrests and convictions of male homosexuals, but few arrests and no convictions of females, even though female homosexuality was widespread. To this day, although some women insist their homosexuality is a legitimate and respectable sexual preference, the female homosexual is much more likely to be viewed as pathetic rather than sinful, immoral or sick.

It is important to realize that our tradition does not speak for all of the people of the world. Cross-cultural studies make it entirely clear that even though homosexuality is always a minority preference, it is viewed very differently in different societies. Some condemn it, others tolerate it and still others have esteemed it or even required it at certain stages of life or among certain select individuals. The ancient Greeks who influenced our own tradition in so many ways did not condemn the love, including sexual love, of young male heroes. If our sexual traditions were based upon other traditions and societies, our attitudes toward homosexuality would be very different indeed.

In eight states now, no sexual behavior between consenting adults in private is defined as criminal. In many states there is far less tendency to prosecute individuals on grounds of private homosexual behavior and there is now far less police time being devoted to entrapping homosexuals. Most mental health specialists view homosexuality as an adjustment problem requiring psychological help; and as yet a minority but growing psychiatric view is that as in the Greek and other traditions, homosexuality is a legitimate and prospectively healthy sexual preference. On the other hand, it is not possible to make accurate statements about "our society's view" of homosexuality. Certainly homosexuals are now far more likely to be viewed as human beings, albeit erring, than they used to be. I have noted changes in attitude toward homosexual leaders who have addressed my classes in recent years which may reflect rather widespread attitudinal changes in society at large. When the first speaker was revealed as a self-avowed homosexual, perhaps the prominent class reaction was surprise that it would not have been possible to distinguish him from any one else. He was "manly" in appearance and voice, had no distinguishing verbal or movement mannerisms or other stereotypes to label him. He was obviously human. Later on, classes began to take humanness for granted but still to react as they would to any speaker for an unpopular cause such as communism, South African racism or such like. Gradually there emerged a dominant view disconcerting to some homosexuals who might be looking for a fight, namely: "Do your own thing. It's nobody else's business."

Now, of course, my students are not a typical American group from which generalizations can be made. However, since the subject can now be talked about much more openly and objectively, and since the popular news media and certainly popular entertainment have been willing to deal with the subject, homosexuals are more likely now to be perceived as human beings with the same rights as other citizens. Homosexual leaders protest that discussions and entertainment involving homosexuality are too much under the influence of the prevalent homosexual stereotype of today—and the homosexual necessarily comes out looking either sick or silly. In other words, they believe that homosexuals are a special group and like other special groups they bear the onus of stereotyping which conceals the individual. We do not deal with most people during the day on the basis of whom they intend to sleep with that night.

In brief, traditional attitudes toward homosexuality are still very much with us and are backed by accepted public morality and, in most states, the law. On the other hand, there is a growing humanistic view which perceives homosexuality as being a private rather than public concern that is like left-handedness: a more difficult but still manageable way of dealing with life.

Question: How common is homosexuality?

Answer: Accurate figures cannot be given. Usually the Kinsey data is still cited for an approximation even though that information is not really representative of the country. Perhaps four percent of the population is assumed to be exclusively homosexual in actual sexual participation, but when account is taken of individuals who are sometimes homosexually involved, have been for an appreciable period of time or who would by preference be homosexual if given the right circumstances, a figure of something like ten percent of the population is defensible. A higher figure may be cited for particular groups. For example, something approaching fifty percent of males who have not married by age thirty-five have or have had appreciable homosexual experience. Perhaps the important point for sex educators and counselors to bear in mind is that in any particular group of individuals a certain percentage are likely to be homosexual by preference. Moreover, a certain percentage are likely to be bisexual, that is, both heterosexual and homosexual.

Question: Is homosexuality inherited?

Answer: Homosexuality has been explained in many ways. It has been claimed that this preference is due to the individual's having the body of one sex but the soul of the other. Also it has been claimed that genetic factors determine homosexuality and make the behavior inevitable. Such theories lack supporting evidence and are no longer accepted as valid explanations.

Question: Are body type or physical mannerisms indications of homosexuality?

Answer: No. Males with broad hips and other so-called female characteristics are no more likely to be homosexual than men of other body builds. Conversely, females with athletic type body builds are no more likely to be homosexual than other females. It is simply a mistake to presume homosexuality—or heterosexuality—on the basis of body structure.

The same is true with bodily movement mannerism. True, a relatively few homosexuals make a studied attempt to conform to the male and female homosexual stereotypes. But, generally speaking, movement characteristics are merely those learned as a child on the basis of imitating older persons' movements. When a boy is described as moving, running or throwing "like a girl," or a girl is described as moving "like a boy," implications may be drawn concerning homosexuality. Actually, ineffective bodily movement has nothing to do with one's sex but with one's knowledge of how to move the body efficiently. In other words, running with toes pointing in and elbows out with hands bouncing is not "female running," it is running with faulty body mechanics—just as efficient running on the part of the female is not "masculine running" but running with good body mechanics. Throwing a ball with the right hand while stepping forward with the right foot is not "female throwing" but inefficient throwing. In other words, inefficient body movement is learned and is correctable in the interest of improved fun and effectiveness in play, sport and so forth. Derogatory labelling of homosexuality is pointless if not vicious.

Question: What does cause homosexuality?

Answer: Students of the subject generally seem to agree that homosexual preference is due to early life experiences which are not positively known. One theory holds that a domineering mother and "weak" father influence creates homosexuality. However, one boy may have a brother who grew up under the same circumstances and did not become homosexual.

It is known that human beings are potentially able to respond sexually to a wide variety of stimuli, just as they may express a basic sense of rhythm in a wide variety of ways. Both human and animal studies show that when the sexes are segregated, sexual interest finds increasing expression with individuals of the same sex. For example, individuals in prisons and institutions which are usually sex-segregated have no choice but to abandon sexual interest entirely or to express it in masturbation or homosexual contacts. Similarly in countries where the young are segregated a great deal and go to separate schools or the girls go to no schools at all, masturbation, homosexuality and prostitution are the only outlets available.

In other words, under virtually any circumstances a certain percentage of individuals will manifest homosexual interest for reasons which may not be apparent. On the other hand, circumstances can certainly encourage the cultivation of homosexual interest.

Spokesmen for the so-called gay community are likely to become very impatient, if not indignant, over this whole question. They argue that we don't really know what causes heterosexuality so why make a great to-do over the equally ambiguous question of what causes homosexuality? Why make a great commotion over the question of why someone likes beef but not lamb or poultry but not fish? Why not, they argue, accept the preference as a fact of no greater significance and respect the individual's right to cater to his preferences.

Question: Is it wise to encourage or ignore evidence of homosexual tendency in the young?

Answer: Let us assume for the moment that the alleged homosexual tendency is real and not merely, for example, physical expression of affection or friendship which is acceptable in some societies but not in ours. It would be difficult to justify encouraging a child to become left-handed in our society if the option of becoming right-handed is available to him. This is a right-handed world, with virtually everything designed for the right-handed person.

Similarly, this is a heterosexual society which tends to

be far more than just inconvenient for the homosexually inclined. The heterosexual individual, almost no matter what he does sexually, is likely to feel far less pressure from a disapproving even hating society, is far less likely to have his sexual preferences held up as reasons for employment discrimination, is far less likely to be ostracized, ridiculed and persecuted than is the homosexual. Still, left-handedness is strong enough to lead a considerable number of people to brave the inconvenience of living in a right-handed world and homosexual preference is strong enough to lead a sizable proportion of the human population to accept the disadvantages of homosexuality in the hostile environment created by the customs, morals and laws of their society.

Question: Is it better for fathers and mothers to discontinue kissing and close physical play with their children of the same sex after early childhood? In other words, might a father's continuing to kiss a son affectionately encourage him to become homosexual?

Answer: This is evidently not a matter of great concern among mothers, but it is a very real cause for concern among a great many fathers. There seems to be no evidence whatever that physically expressing affection by the father encourages homosexual tendencies in the son. On the other hand, many of us have known of a good many cases in which the father's anxiety about this possibility has led him to withdraw physical expression of affection for his son and has upset him very much. As a result, the son has been forced to wonder what he has done or otherwise worry about why his father no longer seems to like him or love him. If the child is having adjustment problems of other kinds at this same time, the addition of this feeling of separation from the formerly affectionate father can be devastating or at least much more difficult. The boy, especially if he is a member of some special group, may find the sudden loss of the supporting, formerly reliable friend all but unmanageable. "When should I stop kissing my son," one speaker was asked. "Oh, perhaps when he gets to be around sixty-five or so," was his answer.

Question: What is the prevailing medical attitude toward homosexuality?

Answer: It would be a mistake to assume that there is a uniform medical attitude toward homosexuality, or that it would be possible to predict the response of a physician to a situation involving homosexuality. Generally speaking, medical training does not take this subject into account. However, it is safe to say that the vast majority of physicians currently view homosexuality as a form of illness possibly requiring psychiatric treatment. Many would refer to it as deviant and possibly immoral behavior. In other words, most physicians can be expected to reflect the traditional views of homosexuality but, perhaps, with the overtones of the recently emerged humanistic rather than persecutory attitude in evidence.

Four major points of view in addition to the more traditional ones seem in evidence among therapists today: (1) Homosexuality is like any other non-reproductive sexual activity engaged in willingly and privately by adults, namely a matter of personal preference which is no one else's business; (2) Sexual preference of the patient is none of the doctor's business, but sexual dysfunction is. In other words, when William Masters 'treats" a homosexual it is not with the intent of curing him of homosexuality but of treating him for problems of homosexual sexual dysfunctioning; (3) Homosexuality is basically a deviation from bio-evolutionary determination and therefore, by definition, evidence of severe mental health problems. In other words, some leading psychiatrists' interpretations of the evidence is that psychological blockage of one kind or another must account for a strong sexual preference that flies in the face of species survival; (4) Finally, the "homosexuality means psychological sickness" view of some psychotherapists based on the cultural-anthropological perspective; that is, homosexuality reflects both psychological disturbance and causes or deepens psychological disturbance, not for moral or biological reasons but because it is so blatantly and violently counter to our steadfastly anti-homosexuality tradition. In other words, such therapists are aware that the ancient Greeks, among others, could esteem and respect homosexuality and not be made sick by it and that many "primitive" peoples of the world have freely and comfortably practiced homosexuality at least under certain prescribed circumstances without ill effect, but they do not consider this possible in our particular anti-homosexual society. However, in very recent years, as homosexuals have been coming boldly forth to assert their rights as human beings and citizens, some psychotherapists believe the societal attitude is being changed. The homosexual is becoming more able to function comfortably, psychologically, than was previously possible.

Question: What about attitudes of therapists and other professionals concerned with special groups toward homosexuality among members of special groups?

Answer: It is not possible to generalize any more because there is a lack of consensus. Probably the majority continue to fight it, to stamp it out along with masturbation. However, a growing number of professional people do not automatically consider the interest or behavior automatically bad. Rather, they attempt to determine the likely consequences of the behavior before passing judgment on it.

If homosexual interests can be expressed under circumstances in which the special group member is not going to be injured, rejected or arrested and if others, such as his family members, are not going to be rejected or otherwise hurt and if the behavior merely brings a degree of warmth and enjoyment to a limited and restricted life—then homosexual relationships are viewed by some professional people as being "good" rather than "bad." Such circumstances and such attitudes are occasionally encountered, for example, in a few institutions where sex segregating is practiced and the only possibility of sex with another person is homosexual.

Question: What is the attitude of the clergy toward homosexuality generally, and toward homosexuality among special group members?

Answer: It is not possible to generalize about this either. Certainly clergymen inclined toward a fundamentalist view would be anti-homosexual under any circumstances. Some clergymen who are generally liberal in such matters as contraception and sexual experimentation among married couples remain quite fundamentalist with regard to specific behaviors, such as masturbation, pornography and homosexuality. Still, there has certainly been a trend in recent years toward a more relaxed attitude on the part of the clergy toward homosexuality. Clergymen are far less likely to view homosexuality as a sin than as an unfortunate behavior due to some maladjustment or as purely and simply a sexual preference. Thus, an attitude of tolerance, acceptance and a desire to be helpful if needed have become increasingly noticeable.

As with doctors and other professional persons, clergymen need to be sounded out on an individual basis with regard to their attitudes toward homosexuality among special group members. One of fundamentalist inclination might be surprisingly lenient because the special group member seems to be such a special case that the usual rules don't apply. On the other hand, a liberal clergyman might be more concerned about this behavior among special group members than he is among others. Generally speaking, however, the clergy's view of homosexuality has become increasingly liberal and helpful, including helping the anxious homosexual work out a happier adjustment to his homosexuality.

Question: Does homosexual seduction early in life give rise to permanent homosexual preference?

Answer: This is usually not the case. However, it might happen, particularly if heterosexual contacts are either not made or are unpleasant. If the individual is encouraged toward homosexuality and discouraged from hetero-sexuality, it is not surprising that his preference may be molded in the obvious direction. However, things are usually not all that simple. For example, some exclusively and very happy heterosexuals report that their early hetero-sexual contacts and experiences generally were very un-pleasant and even extremely painful in one way or another and it took years to work out a happy heterosexual relation-ship. Similarly, some exclusively homosexual individuals report having gone through excruciating initiations into homosexuality—as one well-known writer put it about him-self, he couldn't sit down for a week after his first seduction and the whole experience disgusted him. But with deter-mination he finally became exclusively homosexual, even though the option of heterosexuality was readily available to him. Some individuals who have been seduced homo-sexually have later discovered heterosexual gratification and have gone on to what they consider to be a happy bisexual adjustment which permits equally enjoyable relationships with men or women.

Question: Is homosexuality "curable?"

Answer: In the first place, this question is objectionable to many because it implies that homosexuality is a disease—which it may or may not be defined as, depending on the therapist. So perhaps the question might better be phrased: Can homosexual preference be changed to heterosexual? It is well known that when the sexes are segregated, as in prisons and institutions, there is a sharp rise in homosexual behavior, there being no other form of social sex available. However, when such people are returned to a heterosexual setting, homosexuality is usually promptly abandoned.

So-called fixated or exclusive homosexuals are not readily changed and indeed are likely to insist that they have no more desire to change than do most heterosexuals wish to be changed to homosexuals. Although some formerly exclusive homosexuals have changed and have reported great relief from the stigma of homosexuality, generally, efforts to change have met little success.

Within the last few years, greater public tolerance if not acceptance of homosexuality has probably reduced the psychological stress usually associated with this sexual preference. If this more tolerant attitude continues, homosexual behavior will undoubtedly be associated with far fewer mental health repercussions.

Question: What are prevailing attitudes toward homosexual behavior among special group members?

Answer: Attitudes are conflicting. The most puritanic behavior is likely to be expected of the special group members. Any deviations are likely to be attributed to the individual's specialness, his physical or mental handicaps, aging, etc. Every effort is made to insure that special group members are prevented from giving expression to any homosexual inclinations they may have. In back wards of mental hospitals, the extent to which any such behavior is combatted is sometimes amazing.

The special group member, if not destitute, is likely to enjoy a status which tends to exempt him from the usual rules, at least to some degree. A certain sympathy, however condescending, may protect the "old maids" living together, the physically handicapped (more so than the mentally handicapped whose problem may be viewed as stemming from sexual "deviance") and the affluent aging whose homosexual interests are fairly well accepted.

In settings where special group members are segregated by sex, all forms of sexual expression have been fought by the authorities. Homosexual liaisons have certainly not been exceptions. However, just as masturbation is sometimes viewed as a harmless pleasure which should not be denied to anyone, homosexual expression is sometimes considered better than nothing and ignored. As noted elsewhere, it may even be viewed as part of a worthwhile human relationship which may also include friendship, tenderness and real consideration for another. This kind of permissive attitude does not seem to be widespread as yet but in a quiet way it is probably spreading as people raise questions about the consequences of behavior rather than automatically condemning behaviors because they have been traditionally labelled "bad."

In conclusion. Homosexuality continues to be one of our society's major sexual taboos. Still, it is much more likely to be considered a sickness than a sin, and it is less diligently persecuted than it used to be. Even its status as a sickness is being challenged today. Special group members are likely to be especially carefully scrutinized for this as other sexual behaviors. However, under certain conditions they may be granted a degree of leeway not generally afforded. Still, if justification is being sought for according special group members restricted or even punitive treatment, evidence of homosexuality will almost certainly be used against them.

Perhaps the basic point about homosexuality is that it is not the behavior itself that is considered damaging. Rather, it is persecution of the behavior that is damaging. No one has so far demonstrated that sexual stimulation of or by a member of one's own sex rather than of the other sex is intrinsically harmful. Heated arguments continue over the question of whether varieties of heterosexual sexual experimenting are healthy but the same behaviors performed homosexually are unhealthy, if not sinful and immoral. If homosexual or any other behavior is socially frowned upon and persecuted, the individual engaging in it is not really dealing so much with behavior as with societal attitude toward it. As already pointed out, this is why some mental health specialists fully aware that homosexuality is not intrinsically evil continue to argue against it because of the likely devastating effect of the persecutory societal attitude. Thus the question becomes, in weighing the assets and liabilities of homosexual behavior, do the benefits to life as it is available to the individual outweigh the disadvantages? In some cases, where special protection or privacy is provided, the benefits may prevail for special group members. Usually this is not the case.

CHAPTER 15

INCESTUOUS WISHES AND BEHAVIOR

Incest is one of the most widespread and oldest human taboos. When sexual relationships occur between members of the immediate family, such as between father and daughter, mother and son or sister and brother, it is referred to as primary incest. The word incest may also refer to sexual relationships among cousins or even more distantly related individuals, and in some states marriage is forbidden among varieties of relationships. Among some primitive and modern peoples, royal family members are considered above marriage or sexual activity with members of lower classes. This tradition has given rise to an acceptance of incest on an institutionalized basis. However, this forbidden behavior is generally abhorrent in our society and gives rise to great consternation when it is discovered. Outside investigators in Appalachia were shaken to find in some communities girls of eleven to thirteen were typically introduced to sexual intercourse by their fathers.

In the face of general societal condemnation of incest, close family relationships which bring together members of the opposite sex very commonly give rise to sexual interest. This may or may not be repressed into the unconscious, depending upon how repugnant the situation is to the individual. For example, one brother was conscious through much of his late childhood and early youth of a strong desire to have sexual intercourse with his mother. His brother, living in the same close-knit environment, was never aware of such a wish but occasionally had dreams about his mother in which there were definite but unrecognized sexual overtones. Freud's teachings about the

Oedipus complex indicate that it is a universal step in psycho-sexual development; it gives rise to intensive psychological con-flict, and has as a major complement intense competition of the child for the parent of the opposite sex. It is not necessary to read Freud to be very much aware that seductive behavior between mother and son and father and daughter is extremely common within the dynamics of family life generally.

Much has been written about the incest taboo, and many efforts have been made to explain its existence on a near universal basis. For example, it may have helped to preserve the family by reducing rivalry among family members. However, there is really no way of knowing just how or why it got started. The task is to accept the widespread fear of incestuous wishes and behaviors and to make some kind of objective sense out of them.

Question: What harm is done by incestuous wishes or behaviors?

Answer: Mainly psychological. In those relatively rare situa-tions in which a child is conceived, genetic flaws may be concentrated in the child, but its worst problems are likely to be related to the psychological dynamics. In isolated situations, inbreeding of relatives for extended periods may give rise to deformities which come to typify the entire group.

In the Oedipus myth, Oedipus and his mother were evidently quite happily married and had their children without personal or social difficulties until they and their subjects became aware that they were indeed mother and son as well as husband and wife. Similarly, if a brother and sister were to become separated as infants and then without their or anyone else's knowledge of their relationship, they were to meet and become sexually involved, to marry and to have children, there is no reason to suppose that their unknown incestuous behavior would cause them difficulty, only that their chances of having a defective child might be increased to some extent. However, should they never have children they would doubtless have as happy a relationship as any other couple. Should the biological relationship become known, then the awful incest taboo would likely make itself felt. Oedipus' wife, Jocasta, hanged herself, and Oedipus gouged out his eyes. Modern violators of the taboo would probably not go to such extremes, but the relationship as lovers or as husband and wife would certainly be thrown into jeopardy. Clearly, the ill effect would be psychological and due not to evil consequences of the behavior but to the black magic of the taboo.

Question: What are the effects of undiscovered incestuous relationships within families?

Answer: Of course the literature on abnormal psychology is full of cases in which there are parent-offspring or brother-sister involvements. Certainly such involvements indicate that those involved do not hold their society's customs, morals or laws to be inviolable. Thus the behavior may represent a pattern of nonconformity, just one element within such a pattern, which is likely to be labelled psychopathological.

However, within reasonably well-adjusted families, when incestuous relationships do occur but do not become known to others, the consequence is likely to be severe guilt on the part of one partner or both. For example, as one very bright well adjusted young woman wrote:

"Also at the time I was profoundly uneasy about masturbation, and sex in general—from my parents' own ambivalence about sex, a nurse's punishment of my masturbatory bathing activity, and from guilt reactions to participating in sexual activity with one of my brothers who bribed me with money, comics or the like (the problem was not only that this was—heaven forbid—incest, but also, God help me, that I had enjoyed it and then repressed the whole, unacceptable mess)."

The guilt feelings associated with these childhood experiences should not be underestimated because they contribute greatly to the self-depreciation, fascination with but dread of sex and generally poor self-concept that earlier masturbatory guilt has already established. These sex and self-depreciation attitudes may have made themselves felt continuously during the growing-up period and into marriage where they blocked happy sexual adjustment, until sex education and counseling made possible an objective reassessment of the entire situation. Incidentally, insofar as this young woman knew, her brother experienced no serious psychological or other repercussions for his violation of the incest taboo. It was merely something that he had succeeded in getting away with.

Question: In some societies parents quiet their upset children by fondling their genitals. Is this considered incest?

Answer: No. This is more on the order of taking an infant to the breast or giving it a bottle or even kissing it as a way of diverting it from unpleasant feelings for tranquilization.

Question: How should parents deal with seductive or sudden erotic behavior on the part of their children?

Answer: When such things occurs—and in reasonably close family relationships they are almost bound to at one time or another—the first rational step is to remain calm. If one becomes panicky or otherwise terribly upset he is very likely to make a big thing out of something which need not be traumatic to anyone. The parent can be aware that the offspring's behavior is no more evil or dreadful than seductive behavior on the part of a neighbor or secretary. But he also should be aware that as with neighbors and secretaries it is usually a very poor idea to get involved. One may be flattered that he is attractive to other adults or to a child. But he had better calmly but firmly though nonpunitively move things in another direction. After all, the parent is almost always in complete control of the situation if he or she wants to be.

Question: What about the case of an older strong son forcing his sexual attention upon mother or sister?

Answer: The mother or sister has to make a decision as to

whether it is better to go along with the sexual desires of the young man and accept the risk of all of the personal and social repercussions built into the situation or to call for outside help. In our society, our bodies are supposed to be inviolate. Most sane men keep their hands off young girls because they know that punishment for statutory rape is likely to greatly outweigh any gratification they might obtain from "robbing the cradle." Similarly, people do not have to put up with sexually aggressive relatives. And such relatives tend to get this point very quickly when confronted with it.

Question: Is sexual activity other than coitus considered incestuous?

Answer: Of course this is a matter of definition and context. Vaginal intercourse between relatives under any circumstances is bound to be considered incestuous. On the other hand, a close, loving relationship between close relatives is likely to be considered incestuous whether or not there is evidence of any kind of sexual contact including vaginal intercourse. As noted earlier sexual stimulation may be used for the nonsexual purpose of soothing an upset infant or child. Some concerned and loving relatives of some members of special groups feel duty bound to help their loved one overcome sexual frustration and gain a gratification in life by whatever means will help—usually by facilitating masturbation. In cases of this kind, the incest taboo has simply not seemed relevant or important.

Question: What special implications are there for incest and special group members?

Answer: In brief, the typical negative attitude toward disabilities will simply have the strongly negative attitude toward what is interpreted to be incest added to it. A causative relationship between the condition and the behavior might very well be suspected. In one recent case, a mother was urged by an advisor to abandon her practice of tussling with her two boys, including one who was somewhat "hyperactive." It was argued that such play would encourage incestuous desires which might be especially evident in the boy with the special problem. The mother stopped such physical play, the "normal" child was disappointed but quickly shifted his interests to other of many activities available to him. However, the hyperactive boy seemed very upset because he thought that his mother's attitude toward him had changed. Moreover, his upset continued, perhaps because there were far fewer things for him to turn to as substitute behaviors. Dread of the incest taboo tended to make it extremely difficult for this woman to evaluate the situation objectively, and in attempting to escape it, she left her boy unhappy, bewildered and somehow to blame for his mother's change in attitude towards him. However, with counseling the mother soon decided that there had probably not been any serious sexual overtones in their play and that should there be, she could easily maintain control over the situation. Incidentally, the handicapped child may very well manifest greater curiosity about bodies and various body parts than the average child. This may be due to lack of earlier exposure than most to such things, and to lack of opportunity to make such natural interest conform to socially acceptable expressions.

In conclusion. Difficult as it may be, if and when incestuous interests are noted or suspected, it is good to avoid reacting as though it were some black magic. Rather, it is better to try to evaluate the situation in terms of its meaning. Very possibly, the child's interest in breasts or genitals may very well have been generated not by an impulse to have sexual relations—which the child would very probably not know how to accomplish anyway—but rather to interest aroused concerning what's under all that clothing. Bodies and their parts, such as eyes and fingers, would sometimes appear to be of intrinsic interest to fellow human beings and the inaccessible parts might give rise to special interest. Perhaps a more relaxed attitude toward some degree of nudity in the home would tend to minimize excessive curiosity.

When incest is known to have occurred in a particular situation, it tends to attract considerable attention. Sometimes the impression is given that this is an extremely widespread behavior. Actually, it is not. Observations of both primates and human beings tend to suggest that incest rarely occurs among close family members. Young monkeys play and fight with family members, but sexual arousal is much more likely to occur in connection with individuals outside the family. Similarly, in the communal communities of Israel, boys and girls are likely to be reared on most intimate bases which may include a good deal of nudity together as in bathing, but the individuals almost always turn away from these "brother" and "sisters" for their romantic interest. Also in university coed dorms, males and females tend to feel that they benefit from sharing the intimacies of daily living morning, noon and night, but dating and romantic interest tend to be expressed outside this circle of living mates. These examples of turning away from what may be termed possible incestuous relationships does not mean that primates and human beings possess an inborn "morality" which forbids incest. On the contrary, it seems to mean that sexual attraction is more likely to occur among individuals with whom the mundane circumstances of daily living are not so fully shared.

As with other groups, behavior interpreted as incestuous among special groups is best not reacted to as though a catastrophe had struck. Highly emotional reactions and verbalizations can make the most innocent behavior seem dreadful and can quite unnecessarily give rise to self-incrimination, feelings of loss of love and other detrimental ideas. Should behavior of the special group member be clearly and definitely incestuous in nature, this is not necessarily any worse nor need it be the basis for incrimination or self-incrimination any more than any other erotic feeling which simply cannot be permitted to be expressed. For example, very young girls often behave seductively toward and give rise to erotic feelings in older men. But unless the man wants to get into a great deal of trouble with the law, he enjoys the feelings and perhaps the fantasies about the episode and lets it go at that. Similarly, incestuous arousal is not intrinsically harmful but the rational and responsible person will recognize the inherent dangers in permitting feelings to be acted out and carefully avoid them.

Presumably an occasional parent does what it is necessary to do to help an individual achieve sexual gratification when an injury or other problem prevents achieving gratification alone. Not uniquely, the sister of a crippled young man would help her brother as needed to masturbate successfully. It would perhaps be possible to stamp the black label of incest on such behavior. However it would seem pointless to do so, and it would certainly be a distortion of the intent of the behavior.

CHAPTER 16

CHILD MOLESTATION

CHILD MOLESTATION tends to be a highly emotionally charged term which suggests serious physical and/or emotional damage to a child. Actually, however, it usually involves exhibitionism (the exposing of the male genitals) or more commonly, a touching by hand of the girl's genitals or breasts. Such exposures and contacts tend to be of very short duration and do not lead to coitus, mouth-genital contact or physical injury. The well publicived molestation that leads to or involves physical violence and injury or even death is actually very rare. Such acts of violence are performed by very disturbed individuals and are in a completely different category from the usual forms of "molestation."

Studies of molested girls have shown that: the molester was usually known to the family, perhaps a friend, relative or neighbor; the girls were not forced or injured but perhaps bribed; the girls sometimes initiated or at least encouraged the behavior with esteemed adult males; and there was no evidence of emotional trauma brought about by these experiences. Most molestation went undetected. Of that detected, little is reported to the police because the offender is known to the parents. Parents who make a great to-do about such episodes, emotionally proclaiming the harm done to the child, do risk seriously upsetting her, leading her to believe that she has indeed been injured most seriously.

In some cases the molester is a boy not a great deal older than the girl or girls involved. In one such case, several parents were alerted to the fact that a thirteen-year-old was getting younger neighborhood girls to go to his home while his parents worked. There he "felt them up" and in some cases partially undressed them. The outraged neighbors confronted his parents with his behavior, whereupon severe punishment including complete isolation from other children was inflicted, and no one in the neighborhood would speak to him.

One of my students was impressed by the extreme reactions of the little girls' parents and the boy's father, and by the apparent willingness, even eagerness, of the girls, including his own sister, to be "molested" by this boy. He therefore renewed his friendship with the boy, talked and played ball with him, and thereby very possibly prevented serious emotional damage to the boy who had soon begun to show the effects of being anathematized.

Molestation may take various forms. It may range from "accidental" touching of the girl's body to open efforts to find opportunities to caress breasts and genitals or buttocks. The suddenness of the episode may startle the child but often, contrary to stereotype, it is gentle and non-threatening. A small gift may be given to encourage cooperation. (Some shrewd little girls have learned to capitalize on this gift-getting potential of cooperation.) The victim may be neither revolted nor indifferent. One mother was completely nonplussed to discover that her husband, when more or less drunk, would climb into bed with their two early teenage daughters and play with them sexually, but also that the daughters greatly enjoyed these episodes. Similarly, one young woman from a large well-to-do family told me that uncles and older cousins had never missed a chance to catch her alone at family gatherings, to kiss her and "feel her up" freely—and that she had enjoyed these episodes a great deal, felt flattered by them and sought them out.

Girls have an advantage over boys in one respect. It is girls who experience the realities of sexually inspired contact from an early age. Boys, on the other hand, generally grow up having their sex lives limited to fantasies, talk and masturbation. This situation is not likely to change soon.

My point in mentioning these non-traumatic instances of molestation is to emphasize that we are not dealing here with something that is necessarily intrinsically evil or injurious. However, it is definitely out-of-bounds behavior, socially and legally, and can mean a great deal of trouble. Perhaps some special group members are especially vulnerable to having the worst possible interpretation placed upon any liberties taken with young girls.

Sexual molestation has sometimes been violent and ghastly beyond words. It is fear of this kind of behavior that has sometimes led schools and communities to build deeply ingrained fears of strangers into community children. In a desperate effort to protect their children, parents and others may terrify them concerning all strangers, particularly if they are in the least bit friendly. And since sexual taboos tend to forbid any kind of frank explanation of what is going on, children are likely to get all kinds of terrifying and perhaps magical ideas about the terror stalking among them. Thus, whatever actual physical damage this rare type of molester may have done to one child, panic reaction in the community may guarantee emotional damage to large numbers of others due to irrational over-reaction. Careful supervision of children in situations like going to and from school and seeing that they do not play in isolated lots, woods and houses are realistic and effective preventive measures.

One of the most subtly upsetting aspects of adult and child sexual contact is that, generally speaking, the adult world forms a kind of united front against sex and sexual expression as far as children are concerned. Thus the child who is usually having no easy time adjusting his interest in sex to the apparently anti-sexual stance of the adult world suddenly finds a member of that adult world actually imposing that which is forbidden or taboo upon him. For example, one woman had always felt badly for having over-reacted as a young girl when on one occasion, her grandfather, of whom she was very fond, attempted to caress her breasts. She immediately ran to her grandmother to protest; her grandmother informed the rest of the family and the grandfather carried the stigma of that rather insignificant incident forever afterward.

Question: Are there implications for special group members with respect to child molestation?

Answer: Of course. As in so many other connections, people tend automatically to tie the behavior in with any physical or mental disability or aging, and thereby react to it especially violently. For example, I have known young women to react almost savagely to the idea of young girls being molested by "dirty old men." But when asked how they'd feel about the same thing being done by younger men, their response was far less violent. Similarly, the mentally retarded male is likely to be especially vulnerable to attack. It is almost inevitable that with crippled individuals who happen to be considered freaks in their particular neighborhoods any action interpreted as molestation will be tied in with their "freakishness."

In conclusion. In most cases, molestation represents the conflict between the male's impulse to touch and feel the female, perhaps especially the budding, not very resisting female and society's view of the non-sexuality and "innocence" of the child. The child's innocence is protected by social attitude and backed by law; and the rational self-preserving adult will seek his "kicks" elsewhere no matter how enticing or willing the young girl may seem or how harmless his caresses. Unfortunately, this recommendation is not likely to be taken very seriously, however realistic it may be for special group members.

VENEREAL DISEASES

W E ARE CONCERNED here only with those venereal diseases which, today, constitute major threats to public health: gonorrhea and syphilis. They are literally epidemic in scope; they involve all levels and segments of society, including the very young or prepubertal, and special groups. The most "suspect" age group, 15 to 24, accounts for about half of new cases.

The increase in VD is commonly attributed to the pill, women's lib and other factors considered to have increased sexual activity in society at large. Thus, the focus of preventive attention is often upon reducing sexual activity. Since most VD is transmitted by sexual intercourse and sex without intercourse, avoiding sex would, indeed, virtually eliminate these diseases. However, from a public health point of view, eliminating VD by eliminating sex is about on a par with trying to eliminate dysentery or other food-transmitted disease by eliminating eating. The public has always been uncooperative in such matters.

The more realistic public health approach is to eliminate or control the specific means and agents of infection. This can be accomplished by available and forthcoming technologies—if realistic, open and frank public education on the subject is instituted.

Typically, however, the langague associated with VD is "dirty" and unusable by nice people, especially, perhaps, by parents and teachers of the young. Consequently, society disqualifies itself from dealing effectively with VD, not viewing it as another, basically manageable, communicable disease but as a moral issue. It has been said that society can tolerate the disease, dreadful as it is, but it can't stand to talk about it. So it spreads virtually unchecked at incredible human and financial cost.

Gonorrhea is the most common of the venereal diseases, about five times more prevalent than syphilis. Early symptoms in the male, pain in the penis and a discharge, make possible quick, effective treatment. However, the infected female may have no symptoms whatever. She may therefore be an unknown carrier of the disease; and she is vulnerable to serious complications, internal damage, perhaps sterility. Antibiotics, in particular penicillin and tetracycline, are effective against gonorrhea. However, due to the fact that recent years have seen the emergence of much tougher strains of gonococcus germs, much larger doses are required for treatment than used to be.

Syphilis, a spirochete infection, is the most serious of the venereal diseases. Its early symptoms, such as a mild rash, may be so minor as to go unnoticed or not taken seriously. If untreated, it then passes to further stages, the later ones of which are not infectious but may involve serious damage to any organs of the body, including the heart and brain. Syphilis may be transmitted through the placenta from mother to fetus. Thus, the infant may die before or after birth, or it may live but be severely damaged by the disease. In its first two stages when its only symptoms may be a nonirritating rash on the genitals or thighs, or one or more painless sores which may soon go away, syphilis is highly contagious. (For example, professional VD workers use extreme caution so as to avoid having discharge from their patients' sores contact them.)

Like gonorrhea, syphilis is treated by antibiotics. In the later stages when tissue damage has occurred, the germ may be destroyed but the damage, e.g., to heart, blood vessels or brain, is permanent.

Question: Can you get VD again after being cured?

Answer: Yes, repeatedly.

Question: Can you have syphilis and gonorrhea at the same time?

Answer: Yes.

Question: What do you do if you suspect infection?

Answer: See your doctor or go to your public health department, hospital, or VD clinic. Help is readily available if you'll seek it out.

Question: Is VD transmitted by sexual intercourse only?

Answer: No. Sexual intercourse is the principal way, but any means whereby infectious discharge can reach moist tissue of the body (e.g., kissing, touching the eyes with fingers carrying infectious material, etc., contact with mouth or anus) are likely to pass along the infection.

Question: Can VD be transmitted via toilet seats, etc.?

Answer: VD germs are very delicate and require a warm, moist environment to stay alive. Consequently, it is generally accepted that toilet seats are not a source of danger. However, recent research has raised a question about this.* It seems that live gonorrhea germs can be recovered from toilet seats, brush handles, door knobs, light switches and towel swatches an hour after contamination. However, it has not been proven that contact with such fixtures actually gives rise to infection. Reasonable caution would seem in order, although the former dread of public facilities is absurd and likely to give rise to neurotic avoidance even in time of great need.

Question: Do condoms provide protection against VD?

Answer: Yes, but only to a limited extent. Infectious fluids associated with sexual intercourse may reach vulnerable skin surfaces other than the penis. Moreover, foreplay involving hand contact before a condom is put on, and mouth-genital and anal contacts may render the condom ineffective as VD protection. Moreover, the condom must be properly used e.g., fully covering the penis and not being permitting to slide partway off, as it commonly tends to, after ejaculation.

---

* *Science News,* vol. 105, April 27, 1974, p. 178.

Question: Are prostitutes safe?

Answer: Call girls and girls in expensive houses are relatively safe because of regular medical check-up and the fact that their clients are prone to be safety conscious. Girls (or male prostitutes) encountered in bars or in the streets are usually far less safe. In fact, there is almost always a risk; that is, a carefully supervised professional who gets frequent medical check-ups may become infected after her check-up and then infect any number of persons before the next checkup. Professionals who work under the aegis of therapists are very unlikely to give VD or get it from clients because both are carefully checked and supervised and usually confine sexual activity to this specialty.

Question: Can underage (usually under 18) people get treatment for VD without parental consent?

Answer: In many states, yes, by law. Efforts aimed at controlling VD are so dependent upon treating it and locating its source that few barriers are permitted to stand in the way of anyone.

Question: Can anything be done immediately after exposure which will reduce chances of infection?

Answer: Scrubbing the exposed area with soap and water can be useful, particularly to the male. However, if in doubt, medical consultation is essential for real protection.

Question: What are implications of VD education for special group members?

Answer: Everything said above applies equally to all special group members who are sexually active with partners who are not "known" to be free of infection. Even known and exclusive partners may in some way become infected, so everyone should be taught to recognize the symptoms. (A female who acquires gonorrhea in some way may not develop an observable symptom, but her partner soon will and its source discovered.) Anyone suspected of VD symptoms should seek medical help immediately, without hesitation or shame—just as he or she would if symptoms were to suggest TB, diabetes or heart disease. VD education is generally very inadequate, and special group members are especially neglected in this regard.

Question: Since gonorrhea and syphilis are so readily treatable by antibiotics, why be concerned about getting them?

Answer: In the first place, damage may be done before symptoms are identified and treated (the female may have no early warning of gonorrhea; and the early symptoms of syphilis soon vanish without treatment). The very sexually active may spread these diseases to many other more or less sexually active people before they are treated. Thus, the VD control effort is greatly complicated via the well-known spreading effect whereby a single person can bring about the infection of dozens of others in a short span of time.

In conclusion: VD is a group of diseases which is epidemic, growing at a rapid rate, a real threat to the sexually active and an enormously expensive (both in human suffering and money) aspects of the general public health picture. It affects and is a threat to all segments of the population, including special group members. Unlike heart disease and cancer, existing know-how could bring it under control; but realistic and widespread education concerning it is lacking. Because of its close association with sex (venereal refers to Venus, goddess of love), it continues to be dealt with as a moral issue more than as a communicable disease problem. Generally speaking, people have not tended to associate special groups with sexual interest or activity at all. Therefore VD education has been particularly neglected for these individuals. With changing attitudes toward the sexuality and rights of special groups, realistic VD education for these groups would appear especially urgent.

CHAPTER 18

PORNOGRAPHY

Pornography (FROM THE Greek meaning whore's writings or depictions) has reference to sexual material which is considered obscene. The word "obscene" has a broader meaning, having reference to what the individual or society considers unacceptable to see, say, touch, hear or otherwise confront. Individuals may define virtually anything that offends them as obscene, be it nudity, brutality, stepping on a worm or even the film that buttermilk leaves in a glass. However, that which is obscene is usually culturally defined and recognized as such by the social tradition. For example, in our society acts of elimination, armpits and by some, acts of violence, are likely to be considered obscene. Certainly "hard-core" pornography, which is usually interpreted to mean depictions of some phase of sexual intercourse, is generally considered obscene. Depictions of sex and of violence are often lumped together in a way that tends to confuse the entire subject.

Societies differ markedly with regard to what they consider obscene, particularly concerning children. For example, in France the depiction of violence such as that which takes place in war movies is not considered suitable for young people. They are not permitted to attend movies portraying for example, wartime violence until approximately fourteen years of age. On the other hand, the French do not consider the details of lovemaking obscene and they therefore place no restriction on the observation of such behavior by children. In contrast, we define sexually explicit material obscene and make elaborate efforts to protect our children from it, but we place no limit whatever upon the extremes to which violence may be carried in material viewable by the young.

The traditional deep-seated dread of sexual material—be it merely nudity or some form of sexual activity—relates to a long-standing belief that such material is highly detrimental to the viewer and to society. Thus, oppressive measures have been considered highly justified for the protection of individual children and youth but also for the vitality, even survival, of the entire society. When Anthony Comstock formulated our postal obscenity laws a hundred years ago, he was merely codifying into law a traditional attitude which had grown out of ancient religious teachings and which had acquired considerable support in medical teaching. After all, what does viewing the pornographic give rise to in young men? It gives rise to sexual feelings which are most likely to find release in masturbation, and what does this imply? It implies disaster for the individual: disease, insanity, death and damnation. It also implies decay of the moral fiber of the society at large. Is it any wonder then that enormous and costly effort has gone into stamping out this pernicious influence upon all that is good in the individual and constructive in society?

In 1970, the report of the President's Commission on Obscenity and Pornography reflected the scientific assessment of the whole subject by pointing out that there is apparently no scientific evidence of what might be called personally or socially damaging effects caused by viewing or reading explicit sexual material. The President of the United States, however, lost no time in disavowing the report of the Commission on traditional grounds, namely that pornography constitutes a major modern pollutant which threatens the welfare of the entire society just as air and water pollution do. A more recent U.S. Supreme Court decision has given rise to widespread crackdowns on pornography. The magical tie-in between depiction of the nude and individual and social health continues to be presumed. The decision of what is to be considered "obscene" and "patently offensive" is to be left to local communities. Except perhaps at university levels, medical prescription is to be virtually required if obscene (frankly sexual) materials are to be used legally. A thriving obscenity racket, high prices and severe penalties for violations are to be expected.

Question: Might not pornographic material give rise to harmful misconceptions about sex?

Answer: Yes, they very well might. For example the males involved usually have very large penises, a fact which encourages the misimpression that only males with very large penises are desirable sexual partners. Similarly the usual very large breasts of the girls may give the impression that such large sized equipment is necessary for sexual attractiveness or enjoyment. Moreover the usual frenetic and athletic types of activity may give those with no other sources of information the impression that this is what sex is all about, and perhaps make it difficult to realize that happy sexual encounters are much more likely to be, for the most part, quiet and gentle interactions. For these reasons, if pornographic material is to be of educational benefit, a qualified educator or counselor should be on hand to assist with its evaluation.

Question: These days most concern about pornography seems to be with regard to children. Are children and youth affected in some special way by viewing nudity and sexual activity?

Answer: Very young children take little or no interest in pornographic material. They seem to view it as they might a picture of a couple of dancers. Of course, if they have been trained to think that nudity is bad, they may react briefly to the nudity but again soon lose interest. This point has been made in the popular showings of erotica in Europe where children have attended regularly. Pictures of audiences show adults studying the pictures with care while the children always busy themselves with something else.

As children become more sexually aware in the adult sense, they become increasingly likely to find certain kinds of pornography sexually arousing. Most people consider this feeling enjoyable and of course it may be utilized to enhance masturbatory experiences.

Working independently, Wardell Pomeroy and I have questioned thousands of people in a way that may shed some light upon at least adult perceptions of how pornography seen in childhood affected them. Rather typically, I have asked groups of adults to raise a hand when I would name the time in life when they had first seen what they considered to be hard-core pornography. Hands go up anywhere between pre-school and late in high school or even college, but the majority of hands go up between the sixth and tenth grades. Somewhere along the line everyone has seen what he considers to be hard-core pornography, although until recently many women complained that they had not had the opportunity to see the stag films that they had heard so much about. My next question tends to be in the form of a challenge, namely: "Now how did it affect you? What did seeing it lead you to do? Did you do anything damaging to yourself? Did it lead you to perform any anti-social act that you recall?"

Many people in these groups have been against pornography, especially for children; but not one person over a period of years has been able to produce evidence from his personal experience that harm resulted.

A few reported having been shocked, but being shocked is hardly tangible evidence of ill effect such as damage to mental health. Pomeroy's findings have been completely in accord with mine, and as a psychotherapist, he must be extremely sensitive to influences which may be damaging to mental health.

(On one occasion I was pleased to have a college student maintain that yes, she did feel that she had been hurt by looking at pornographic pictures. She said that as a little girl, she had been looking at a sexy book when her father saw what she was looking at and said, "Now, Jean, you know I never tell you what you can't read but I am going to ask you not to show that book to your little sister." Jean said that this episode upset her for about a week—because it was her little sister who had given her the book.)

Question: What does 'prurient" mean? The Supreme Court has set as the first criterion of pornography the question of whether it appeals to the prurient interest.

Answer: "Prurient" is a dirty word which people simply assume to mean something very bad. Actually it means itch as in sexual itch and is concerned with whether or not the material gives rise to sexual feelings. Now of course advertisers and entertainers do their very best to appeal to the sexual interest in their efforts to sell their products; and we all seem to rather like this and respond to it unless there is a court case and the witch hunt of prurience is on. If we were really against appealing to the prurient interest, most modern advertising and entertainment would have to be altered almost beyond recognition. One girl in a class threw the entire subject into a different perspective by raising the question, "Well, what is wrong with having your prurient interest appealed to?"

Question: Has society's attitude toward pornography changed in recent years?

Answer: The pin-up girls of World War II convinced millions of men that such things are basically "good" rather than "bad"; and it may be that the respectability of these pictures broke the grip of the Puritan attitude which had previously driven most such material underground. These days it is a rare movie indeed that is censored, and convictions are hard to come by. For example, Mayor Daley of Chicago recently outlawed the film *Deep Throat,* but the ban was immediately lifted by a federal judge. Police in the Midwest complain that they make the arrest but there is not enough public support of censorship to bring about convictions.

I recently served as the guest expert on a television program which was carefully contrived to generate a great deal of strong feeling, angry shouting and vivid reaction from an audience selected to represent extreme views. Try as he would, the M.C. could not ignite a fire. The man who owned two pornographic theatres and claimed to have written 250 pornographic books felt that he had been making an important social contribution and no one cared to challenge him on this point. The conservatives felt that they could protect their children's eyes from undesirable material and certainly did not want any government interference in the matter. My informational comments were received with polite interest; no one cared to challenge the flimsy basis of our censorship laws or the futility of trying to control what people choose to look at or read. In brief, it was a very disappointing program as far as generating controversy was concerned. It was, perhaps, reflective of the rather general indifference to the whole matter—except on the part of high officials and crusading groups groping about for easy solutions to complex social problems.

Still, it is well to bear in mind that many homes, church groups, most schools and all politicians who speak in public are firm believers in the evils of pornography and will continue for some time yet to stamp it out by any possible means. The Supreme Court ruling (1973) will facilitate this effort temporarily.

Question: If pornography is not harmful to individuals or to society, are there ways in which it might be considered beneficial?

Answer: Yes. It can be entertaining, educational and even therapeutic. It can be entertaining to some people in the same sense as other forms of harmless entertainment including art appreciation. Different people are entertained by different things, but of course entertainment by definition finds its validity in subjective judgments.

Of course pornography can be educational in the sense of providing planned and systematic learning experiences directed toward some worthwhile educational goal. For example, so-called pornographic material drawn from historical samples can be shown to represent one of mankind's most ancient and universal preoccupations as it has been preserved in art forms throughout the world. Representations of nude people in various kinds of activities can help people overcome their ingrained revulsion at the sight of the human body in its natural state. Moreover, a great many people can expand their knowledge of coital possibilities by watching experienced individuals demonstrate—just as people who know only the dog paddle in swimming can get all kinds of new ideas by watching films or other depictions of various swimming strokes. Another perhaps more subtle educational value of pornography may be to help bring the whole matter within the realm of human experience rather than being something so apart from life as to be beyond rational management or consideration.

In brief, suitable pornographic material can indeed be therapeutic as well as entertaining and educational, and may sometimes combine all three.

For example, sex counselors have often helped worried people to realize they are indeed capable of sexual arousal by having them look at and/or read good pornographic material. Mates are sometimes taught to help bring their own level of sexual interest into reasonable harmony with that of their partner by means of use of pornographic materials. After all, a partner who has been preoccupied with business or household matters may need considerable help in shifting to a sexual focus of a mate who is already more or less focused upon sexual interest. Creating a sexual atmosphere for maximum enjoyment is not at all different from creating an atmosphere which will encourage maximum enjoyment of a meal together. Under the aegis of professional counselors, some individuals have used pornographic materials to help them learn to masturbate and have thus taken first steps in the directions of overcoming general sexual dysfunction.

Question: Are there special implications of pornography for members of special groups?

Answer: Generally speaking, no. In the foregoing, ample allowance has been made for differences in individual interests and tastes. The nature of the irrational taboo as presented certainly applies to everyone; and the negative stance of the traditional morality which school officials, public officials and to some extent the law certainly apply to special group members as well as to the rest of society.

Still, on at least two counts, members of special groups are in a peculiar position with regard to pornography. In the first place, any interest that they may show in it is likely to be attributed to their handicap rather than to a general human interest. In the second place, the special group member may have been so shielded from the realities of human sexuality that both adjustment to and need for such material may be especially great. For example, a deaf individual who has been led to have very negative feelings towards his or her sexual feelings may be profoundly shaken upon seeing frank depictions of human sexual behavior. On the other hand, his near total ignorance of how to express erotic feelings toward a mate, for example a new wife, may put him in the position of needing all of the help possible, including selected pornographic material, in the interests of working out some kind of satisfactory sexual adjustment.

In conclusion. "Pornography" has been a dirty word for so long and has tended to give rise to such automatic negative responses that perhaps it would be well to use other terminology when considering the possible uses of explicitly sexual material among special group members. For example one might refer to good or poor erotica (from the Greek Eros, the god of sexual love) with respect to a particular use. For example, the film *Like Other People* is a fine film with respect to showing how severely cerebral palsied individuals may be helped to develop a close and independent relationship as they become like other people in their loving enjoyment of each other; but it is poor

---

    ° Didatic Films, Garwich House, Horley, Surrey, England.

erotica in the sense that the couple merely vanishes under the covers when it comes time for the explicit sexual interplay.

In any event, sexual material has its place in the education and counseling of many members of special groups. It would be a foolish mistake to ignore the possible value of such material in the heightened enjoyment of life or the educational and therapeutic possibilities that erotica may hold.

CHAPTER 19

SEXUAL INTERCOURSE AND
SEX WITHOUT INTERCOURSE

SOLITARY SEXUAL ACTIVITY can be very gratifying, tension relieving and relaxing. However, most people are profoundly attracted by the possibiilties of sexual activity with another person. In fact, this attraction along with that of physical play may be among the fundamental socializing impulses of humans. Because of its evolutionary value for species survival, the vast majority of human beings possess what may be called a strong potential to engage in sexual interaction. However, two considerations are of importance in this regard: individuals vary tremendously with regard to the strength of their sex drive; and a strong potential for sexual expression may manifest itself in a variety of ways. These facts apply to members of special groups as well as to the rest of the population.

A major misconception about coition is that people have an instinctive knowledge of how to do it. "Wait till the time comes and you'll know what to do." This is simply not true. Untold marriages and other relationships have lost their potential for sexual happiness because useful education was not supplied when needed.

If sexual intercourse is undertaken for the specific purpose of conceiving a child, the best positioning is probably with the female on her knees and forearms with buttocks somewhat elevated and with the male mounting from the rear ("dog style" or, more politely, "à la vache," French for "cow style"). This positioning utilizes gravity to help encourage pooling of the semen near the cervix, thereby increasing chances of large numbers of sperm penetrating the cervix.

But since people do not usually engage in sex to conceive a child, the question really is, Which of the numerous possibilities are most enjoyable to the particular couple? Thus, just as couples can usually agree upon games that they do and do not enjoy playing together, they can usually agree upon sexual techniques that they find most appealing. Adventuresome couples can usually discover "new" techniques which bring a great deal of gratification as well as variety into their sex lives; but others, like people who confine themselves to tennis or skiing or exclusively to any sport, may be perfectly content to stay with one or a few of the many existing possibilities. Certainly there is merit in exploring various possibilities because unexpected pleasures may result. The human body has a variety of potentially erogenous zones, stimulation of which—before, during, after or even instead of intercourse—may greatly enhance the total sexual experience.*

> Question: Isn't there a natural way in which sexual relations should culminate?
>
> Answer: No. The word "should" is a sleeper in this question. It implies that after all, there is some preordained, true way like a religious ceremony. If pregnancy is being sought, then of course ejaculation ordinarily best occurs deep within the vagina. If, however, the intent of the sexual relationship is pleasure—which it is in the great majority of cases—then it is best for couples to work out for themselves what techniques, positionings and so on are most gratifying. Female lying or squatting on top is a popular position, especially if she is smaller. Male partly on top but carrying most of his weight on his side avoids the female's feeling pinned down or restricted in movement.
>
> Some sexologists believe that the typical American

------

* See A. Ellis, *Art and Science of Love*. New York, Lyle Stuart, 1960. Also in paperback; and A. Comfort (editor), *The Joy of Sex*, New York, Crown, 1970. (Illustrated edition available.) *Sexology* magazine is an inexpensive and valuable aid. (Sexology, Inc., 200 Park Ave. So., New York, N. Y. 10003).

obsession with penis-in-vagina coition is one of the major stumbling blocks in the way of sexual fulfillment for many people; and training of their patients usually begins with exploring especially hand and mouth techniques. These tend to be more amenable to fine control and stimulation in precisely those ways that tend to bring greatest pleasure to the mate. However, two considerations need to be taken into account. Individuals brought up with the notion that any but penis-in-vagina with man on top is a perversion may have some difficulty unlearning this nonsense in order to function in other ways. In the second place, a certain number of women stoutly maintain that deep thrusting of a relatively large penis within the vagina is of the essence and therefore necessary for full sexual gratification.

People in some special groups may well begin their search for sexual enjoyment with the realization that penis-vaginal coition is not a possibility for them but that this is by no means necessarily a handicap. Elderly individuals, the very fat, persons with back or other disabling conditions, persons without feeling in their lower bodies, persons without sex organs capable of functioning in traditional coition, women late in pregnancy or following menopause when the vagina may undergo painful degeneration—all must discover alternative means of relating sexually. And to repeat, the alternatives, such as properly used vibrator, may at least equal the enjoyment of penis-in-vagina coition even among many perfectly capable of coition.

Question: Does sex play best culminate in intercourse?

Answer: As indicated earlier, not necessarily. Although some women find deep penetration of the vagina and vigorous thrusting by the penis most gratifying, others are more or less indifferent to vaginal pentration. In fact, some prefer stimulation of other erogenous zones such as the clitoris, or combination stimulation such as clitoris, breast and anal opening the important things. Mouth, tongue and fingers may very well be far more important means of stimulation than the penis.

For their part, males may find mouth and tongue or

hand stimulation superior to vaginal. Whereas vaginal action and contraction are largely automatic, mouth and hand stimulation can be conducted with precisely the control desired for maximum gratification.

Needless to say, if for any reason penis within vagina intercourse is not possible or wise, gratification requires the using of other techniques which are by no means inferior. Many sex educators, counselors and parents urge the young and others anxious to avoid pregnancy to learn to confine themselves to varieties of non-vaginal intercourse.

Question: But aren't the non-vaginal forms of intercourse considered merely foreplay?

Answer: They are sometimes so described and even justified only on the grounds that they lead to and culminate in penis-in-vagina intercourse. Such a requirement is setting an arbitrary and completely unnecessary criterion of what full, "normal" intercourse should be. Many do consider foreplay merely preparatory. But other couples find their greatest satisfaction in non-vaginal stimulation; and it is pointless to designate alternatives merely preparatory or second best—unless, of course, procreation rather than recreation is the objective.

Question: How often should couples engage in sexual play or coition? For example, is there an optimal number of times per week?

Answer: The word "should" implies that there is some arbitrary standard, which there is not. Frequency is something that needs to be worked out on the basis of personal preference and what is feasible. There is really nothing sacred about having three meals a day, but most people adjust their lives to eating at least this frequently and manage to approach most meals with some degree of enthusiasm even though they could go for several weeks without starving to death. Similarly, people know that they can survive indefinite periods of sexual abstinence but most choose to enjoy themselves on a more frequent basis. Some even set aside specific times for sexual activity just as they do for eating so as to better resist the innumerable pressures which tend to lead to endless postponing of sexual pleasure.

Some sexologists of high qualification and reputation have for years argued in favor of "frequent" sex in the interest of health. For example, a noted psychiatrist, Frank S. Caprio, believes "Sexual, physical and mental health all go hand in hand. Yet, doctors are reluctant to prescribe a healthy sexual outlet for one's well being in the same way that they would prescribe a vitamin, tranquilizer, or sedative."[1] He tries to teach his patients suffering from what he calls "sex sickness" that the "sex-love drive is part of our normal instinct of self-preservation." He lists numerous psychosomatic effects of sex sickness, including nausea, fatigue, insomnia, states of anxiety and depression, colitis, loss of appetite, headache or pains in the chest, etc., as possible symptoms of sexual frustration. He urges all doctors in general practice as well as in psychiatry and other specialties to explore sexual histories for clues as to possible causes of complaints.[2] Of course, it is often not enough merely to prescribe more sexual activity. Counseling of both patient and mate may be required if heightened sexual gratification is indeed to result from such efforts.

Question: What if couples or partners are not sexually "ready" at the same time?

Answer: Unless they have gone through some sexually warming up period together, such as playing or talking erotically, or viewing what is for them attractive erotic material together, there is a very good chance that one or the other will be feeling less sexy. The stereotype situation is for the man to be eager but for the woman's preoccupation with children, what is "proper" time for sex, etc., to lead her to put him off. Perhaps just as commonly, however, the man's preoccupation with his work or with TV may make

---

[1] F. S. Caprio, "Sex: A Doctor's Prescription for Better Health," *Sexology* (May, 1973).

[2] *Ibid.*

sex the last thing on his mind. The all too common tendency in such cases is for the less ready partner to throw a damper on the enthusiasm of the other either by expressing disinterest, fatigue and desire to postpone. In some cases, mates use such occasions to accuse the partner of being abnormally interested in sex, and so forth. Putting off or putting down a partner can easily damage the sexual relationship and perhaps turn interest elsewhere.

Usually, the less interested individual can go along with the desires of the partner, perhaps even feigning enthusiasm at first, only to find that enthusiasm soon becomes genuine and the enjoyment very real. Obviously there are times when putting off sex is necessary. But even then, the thoughtful mate need not feel exploited if he helps the partner achieve sexual bliss alone from time to time.

Question: Should the male initiate sexual activity at least most of the time?

Answer: Here again the word "should," as though there were a divine prescription for such matters. Custom has it that it is the male's prerogative or responsibility to be the initiator of sexual activity. However, this is solely a matter of custom which is best ignored by individual couples. Women tend to have their sexual interests fluctuate with different stages of the menstrual cycle; and most men note less easily explained fluctuations in their libido. Biological rhythms are likely to be overlaid by sexually arousing stimuli of many types in the environment. Thus, it would be highly unlikely if one sex or the other were to feel like being the initiator of all sexual activity—even though just as in everything else, few mates are very precisely matched with regard to basic sexual interest.

The point is that frank and open expression of sexual interest to the mate, regardless of genital sex, is healthy and less likely to give rise to the frustrating and sometimes outrageous misunderstandings, frustrated efforts at seduction, anxiety over proper sex role, and so on.

Question: What can be done when one partner believes that oral, anal and even manual sexual stimulation are dirty, abnormal or unnatural.

Answer: It is not surprising that many people have this view considering the extremely negative attitude of our tradition, toward oral and anal sex relations. This tradition is reflected by the fact that in most states such behaviors are criminal and involve incredibly severe penalties, such as many years in jail. Oral sex has become far more socially acceptable in recent years than it used to be and is widely recommended, even by some of the more conservative clergy as being a legitimate form of sexual play. Ironically, counselors sometimes do not realize that they are advising the breaking of very punitive laws when they make such recommendations.

With reassurance and gentle practice, most individuals become able, if they wish, to experiment with a variety of non-vaginal techniques. On the other hand, many prostitutes report that some of their customers come to them specifically because their wives are unwilling to deviate from "missionary" style.

Finally, some who object to oral or anal sex techniques are not revolted by these but simply cannot or do not know how to manage them. For example, although it is a simple matter to stimulate the penis, including the very sensitive underportion below the glans (the frenulum) with the tip of the tongue, taking the entire penis into the mouth and down into the throat may be physically impossible, at least without a great deal of practice. Similarly, anal penetration, particularly if adequate lubrication is not utilized, can be unpleasant or downright painful. Some males have very short tongues and therefore find oral stimulation of the female genitals most difficult. Moreover, even though some men find female sexual odors highly attractive, others find them unpleasant and nonsexy even after washing. (Female deodorizers may help, but many people are allergic to them.)

In brief, sex counseling may help to overcome "moral" objections to manual and oral stimulation of the body, genitals and perhaps anus; and it may teach facilitating techniques. Manual stimulation becomes popular with most couples with a little practice, as does also mouth and tongue stimulation wherever desired. Anal penetration is very popular among a relatively few.

Question: What about other erogenous zones—that is, parts of the body which when stimulated tend to give rise to sexual feelings?

Answer: As sexual arousal increases, the body as a whole becomes increasingly erogenous. (As Freud said, in arousal, the entire body becomes a sexual organ.) Individuals differ, but the inner thighs, breasts of both male and female, underarms, neck, ears and lower back are common erogenous zones. The pubic area tends to be a major zone. Stroking and caressing of these areas tend to be very gratifying and arousing and are particularly valuable to individuals whose genital structures are dysfunctioning or in need of direct warming up. With many people, these zones are of extreme importance, but not as buttons to be pushed in a perfunctory way. Many a girl has complained that the guy "played with her tits a little, stroked her clit a little and then went right on in for his release," all of this meaning less than nothing to the girl involved.

Question: What about use of a vibrator as a form of stimulation?

Answer: Many females find vibrators an excellent means of sexual arousal. Sex counselors often recommend that women use them on themselves to facilitate sexual release alone, and especially as a means of learning to experience orgasm. It may be considered a training device in preparation for successful intercourse. The male may use it as an effective means of arousing his mate for intercourse or as a means of helping gratify her repeatedly.

Some males need to be taught that the vibrator is an

aid to them, not a competitor. However, there are some males who are so upset by the idea of using a vibrator at all that the approach is best abandoned. Males generally do not find vibrators useful in their own arousal or release, although some may.

Question: Is it normal to have fantasies or vivid sexual imaginings while engaged in sex with someone?

Answer: Check the earlier chapter on normality as a sex problem to recall some of the possible meanings of the word "normal." According to the moral model of normality, it is likely to be abnormal to think much about sex at all. But by the statistical and health models, such fantasies are very normal.

Perhaps the more useful question to raise is, Are fantasies and imaginings helpful in achieving the desired sexual gratification? If so, they might best be considered a part of the environment intended to enhance the erotic experience. They are the artwork of the mind, entirely private (some couples do enjoy sharing their fantasies) and harmless even if they do get pretty wild in terms of involving anything from being "gang banged" or gang raped to having sexual relations with a neighbor, mother-in-law or with some animal.

An old joke raises the question: "What are the heaviest and lightest things in the world?" Answer to what is lightest: "A penis. A thought can lift it." The right thoughts can indeed lift it. This is why some sex therapists attempt to get their patients of both sexes to learn to have vivid imaginings of things that bring about sexual arousal in them. This technique is sometimes helpful in overcoming impotency in the male and lack of response in the female. Fantasies are among the things that may help bring about sexual satisfaction—along with sex pictures and writings, body play and direct stimulation of the genitals.

Question: Is climax (orgasm, coming) necessary for sexual enjoyment and satisfaction?

Answer: Much has been said about the sexual enjoyment of non-orgasmic women, that is, women who greatly enjoy encounters but do not actually reach orgasm. Undoubtedly, the pleasure of giving pleasure, of being held and fondled affectionately and of holding and fondling can be most rewarding. However, most women who have discovered orgasm and especially multiple orgasm very much prefer to include this experience in their lovemaking.

On the other hand, some special group members strive to build a sizeable portion of a rewarding life around sexual gratification that does not include orgasm. Some writers have claimed that *coitus reservatus,* the withholding of orgasm, is especially rewarding for males. They have claimed that high spiritual union, experience beyond orgasm, is available to both males and females who prolong intercourse and linger quietly just short of climax. Some special group members benefit from and profoundly enjoy a quiet approach to sex which capitalizes upon exquisite non-orgasmic sensations which may be built up through, primarily, finger, mouth and tongue stimulation of the body, especially the clitoris and the penis. People with spinal injuries (e.g., paraplegics), heart problems and other illnesses, and older persons, especially males, have found non-orgasmic sex highly satisfying.

Many an older or weakened man has found the mate's educated, vigorous, sensitive "attack" upon the penis with mouth and tongue or well-lubricated hands irresistible in terms of bringing on erection and augmenting sensations. The male's need for exertion is thus greatly reduced if not eliminated. Climax can be avoided as the couple learns to linger at the brink. The man is likely to be eager for frequent episodes of this kind, many claiming that coming reduces the ability to reach high peak experience for perhaps several days.

For her part, the female usually responds best to gentle, sensitive stroking of the clitoris by lubricated finger or by tongue, which brings her to repeated orgasms. Couples may trade off in this activity so as to concentrate on their own sensations and having or avoiding orgasms; but they may also learn to stimulate each other simultaneously in the preferred way.

Males may find it difficult to believe that sex can be most gratifying and fulfilling without orgasm, including ejaculation. However, the experience of a great many men testifies to the fact that it may. Many special group members should know this if they wish to continue an active and enjoyable sex life.

Question: Does sexual release have a weakening effect, for example, on the following day?

Answer: No. Traditional misconceptions which have led coaches to isolate their athletes from members of the other sex including their wives for as much as a week prior to important contests are no longer taken seriously. Even those individuals who move a considerable amount during intercourse expend only a moderate amount of energy. Some couples move very little except perhaps at climax and so of course expend even less energy. Research has validated* the commonplace observation that work capability is not lowered on the day following intercourse. In fact, both men and women are far more likely to describe themselves as having been refreshed, revitalized and made to feel better by sexual activity. Many athletes prefer to avoid intercourse during the hours prior to competition because they find it is too relaxing. However, some over-tense athletes, such as short distance runners and wrestlers, find sexual release an especially valuable means of lowering tension and improving performance.

Question: What are some special implications of sexual intercourse for special group members?

Answer: At a recent meeting on sex education and counseling of the handicapped, I asked a young paraplegic man to comment on the film "Touching" which had just been

---

* W. R. Johnson, "Muscular performance and coitus," *Journal of Sex Research,* 4:247-48, August 1968.

shown. In the film, a paraplegic and his lover are shown enjoying hand and mouth stimulation of each other's bodies but in particular the genital and anal regions. The paraplegic observers' comments pretty well summarized implications for special groups generally. He said that the film was great but that it should not be taken to limit other possibilities available to people. He stressed the importance of locating and cultivating all possible erogenous zones; and he stressed the importance of frequent, joyful practice. He pointed out that because of their care in cultivating their available sensory resources and by virtue of frequent practice, the happiest lovers he knew happened to be a paraplegic married to a quadraplegic.

In brief, members of special groups who wish to include sexual activity with a partner among their pleasures in life may very well need to abandon preconceived ideas of how intercourse is supposed to take place, consider the range of possibilities that exist for them and try them out. Patience, not only with partner but perhaps especially with self, may prove extremely important. That is, just as one often does not cultivate an ear for Beethoven upon first contact, repeated exposure to bodily sensory experience may be necessary as appreciation is developed. It is unwise to demand or even expect instant "success' on the part of either mate or self, and it is certainly a mistake to set this as a criterion. After all, if you are going to learn to play tennis, you had better not declare yourself a failure, rotten and hopeless if you bat a few balls over the fence, plunk a good many balls into the net or have some difficulty at first hitting balls consistently within the playing area.

Special group members who have been sexually active prior to illness, injury, aging, etc., have distinct advantages. They know what they are looking for in sex, what tends to be pleasing to them and so on. For example, a quadraplegic who had been sexually active before injury was completely satisfied that his sex life was unchanged because he had a basis for comparison afterwards.

On the other hand, special group members who want

sexual gratification but do not have the benefit of previous experience can usually be taught. Sex education, counseling and, if appropriate, readings, audiovisual aids, etc., can be extremely valuable in leading to achievement of sexual gratification. People are no longer almost necessarily on their own!

Question: What has been said about sexual intercourse for members of special groups is all very well for those who have willing partners to participate with them. But what about the very large numbers of individuals whose sexual interests are strong but who do not possess partners for sexual exploration and enjoyment?

Answer: As with everyone else, they have to make out as best they can. For some, even masturbation is not feasible without at least the reluctant help of someone else. The question of utilizing trained prostitutes is discussed in Chapter 24 in greater detail. However, *suitably trained* and paid sexual "companions," lover "surrogates" or whatever they may be called, may prove very satisfactory to those able to afford such services. In situations where special group members are segregated sexually, gratification by means of like-sex contacts have been found to be highly gratifying in some cases. However, since sexual expression of many special group members is likely to be frowned upon even more darkly than it tends to be in others, the interested must explore their environments for whatever resources they may contain. As indicated elsewhere, some veterans find their home environments unacceptable and move to foreign countries where sexual and other services are within their means.

In conclusion. Sexual intercourse and/or sex without intercourse can add an important dimension to the lives of many special group members and their mates. Various possibilities exist, and individuals need to experiment so as to discover what is most gratifying to themselves and to their partners. Various positions for intercourse need to be tried; hands, tongue and mouth used on various parts of the body offer a range of possibilities. Restrictions imposed by handicap, illness or aging can usually be compensated for by making fullest use of existing possibilities for bodily "pleasuring" of oneself and one's partner. Orgasmic release ("coming") is not a necessary condition of sexual pleasure. That is, enormous sexual gratification is reported by individuals when spinal injuries eliminate awareness of climax in the usual sense and by older men who maintain a prolonged state of arousal just short of orgasm, deliberately avoiding coming in the interest of frequent high-pitch "seances."

Special group members who do not have cooperative mates must do as virtually everyone else does: seek out what they can, masturbate, appeal to the reason of persons who could help out, even utilize paid sexual companions (who are prepared in advance to work effectively and are checked out for VD) or give up on the whole business and turn to philosophy, drink, fishing, music or what not. These days, chances are improving that the individual will receive understanding and perhaps help in reaching his sexual goals. But one must decide that he would *like* rather than *need* sex with a mate. Otherwise, unless one is wealthy, he or she is likely to be setting himself or herself up to feel terribly frustrated, unhappy and abused. It's great to have intercourse when you want it, but as almost everyone can tell you, you can live without it.

CHAPTER 20

CONTRACEPTION

T HERE IS NO longer much opposition to the idea that children should be conceived only when they are wanted and well prepared for. However, in this country, even brighter and better educated segments of the population, married and unmarried alike, cannot be counted upon to utilize available contraceptive methods when engaging in sex recreationally rather than procreatively. In dating situations, the presumption is, particularly on the part of females, that intercourse is not going to take place and therefore contraceptive measures are not provided for.[1] There is still considerable pressure upon "nice" girls not to expect intercourse especially on first or early dates so that any provision for contraception is left to the male. This unrealistic approach results from the influence of unrealistic societal attitudes. In some countries, notably Sweden, it is taken for granted that healthy young people who have the opportunity are likely to avail themselves of sexual enjoyment. Consequently, contraceptives are readily available to both males and females and the prevailing societal attitude makes it easy for them to provide against pregnancy without raising a question of their moral fiber. Of course the societal attitude is conveyed to them primarily by their families and they simply grow up taking for granted that unless people want babies, they utilize contraception. This attitude is evidently growing in the United States, but the prevalence

---

[1] R. Needle, *The Relationship Between Sexual Behavior and Ways of Handling Contraception Among College Students,* Doctoral Dissertation (University of Maryland, 1973).

of unwanted pregnancy indicates that it is far from universally accepted.

Along with a growing tendency to assume that sexual enjoyment is among the rights of members of special groups, there is an accompanying attitude that such gratification usually needs to be considered in a separate category from reproduction. It is hard to argue that a particular condition should disqualify any individual from seeking sexual enjoyment. But unwanted pregnancy resulting from such enjoyment is often in no one's best interest, and a matter-of-fact approach to contraception education is urgently needed.

Special group members vary a great deal with regard to their need for contraceptive education and use. For example, women beyond the menopause need not worry about pregnancy, but older men whose mates are considerably younger need to be very much concerned. Some spinal injury victims are incapable of pelvic movement, but an active female can easily compensate for this lack and therefore contraceptive measures are needed if unwanted pregnancy is to be avoided. Some mentally retarded individuals are highly fertile, but others such as the Down's Syndrome or mongoloid individuals are very rarely fertile. The need for a highly individualized approach is evident.

Question: What are the most effective methods of contraception?

Answer: There are a number of highly reliable contraceptives, but what is best must be determined on an individual basis. For example, at present the pill may very well be the best contraceptive for a great many women. However, some should not use it for medical reasons. That is, if they have a history of blood clotting or if they tend to develop severe headaches, taking the pill may actually be dangerous for them. The pill is a prescription drug and should be used with careful medical follow-up. Generally speaking, however, it is much safer than pregnancy.

The modern rubber or condom is highly effective if properly used (instruction *is* needed) and it offers a degree of protection against venereal disease. The diaphragm with cream or jelly is also highly effective and if combined with the condom is likely to be one hundred percent effective. The intrauterine device is great for population control, but in individual cases it is best supplemented by other methods such as condom or cream.

Sterilization can be accomplished in both the male and female by simple surgery.* It is best selected by individuals who, for whatever reason, do not want to have children of their own. The procedure is entirely effective. That is, later operations cannot be counted on to restore fertility in the male, and the simple forms of operation in the female are irreversible. It is important to stress that sterilization merely disconnects the sperm or egg ducts. It does not involve removal of the sex glands (testes or ovaries) and is, therefore, not the same as castration. Many follow-up studies have shown that it does not reduce sexual interest or ability (although it may in lower animals, such as mice). For those who have as many children as they want, do not want children of their own at all, or who are judged incompetent to function as parents because of severe retardation or other reasons, sterilization provides complete protection without interfering with recreational sex. Most doctors are able to make the necessary referrals for the operation. Planned Parenthood is a good source of guidance on the subject and of referrals to qualified specialists.

Question: When should sexually active young people begin using contraception?

Answer: This is not the simple question it may appear to be. In general, it is probably wise to consider the approach of puberty as the time when pregnancy is possible. However, since ovulation may begin some years before puberty, pregnancy is a possibility then. Much more commonly, ovulation does not begin until several years after the onset

---

* Medical and legal issues associated with voluntary and involuntary sterilization, especially of minors, may be found in J. Robitscher, *Eugenic Sterilization,* Springfield, Thomas, 1973.

of menstrual periods (menses). Consequently, it is at present not really possible to say when any given girl might become capable of conceiving. A simple saliva test may presently become available which will show whether pregnancy is possible. In one case, a ten-year-old girl had a baby and the family calmly raised it as though it were its mother's sister. (The neighbors who had been well aware of the little girl's pregnancy were remarkably cooperative in treating the girls as sisters, and the illusion of a "normal" family relationship was maintained.)

Some special group members may be sexually active at a very early age. For example, little girls may learn very early that their sex is one of their main sources of appeal to available males. In another type of situation, pre-pubertal girls in a residential school for mentally retarded made out very well financially by charging ten cents a "trick" for meetings in the back of the library. Their particular business came to the attention of the principal when a group of boys complained to her that the girls had raised their prices. In such situations, if sexually mature males are about, pregnancy is almost bound to occur if contraception or rigid segregation is not practiced.

Question: Are there special implications for contraception counseling and education for members of special groups?

Answer: There are likely to be. For example, educators and counselors may very well need to take into account what may be unusual degrees of individual differences in needs and capabilities. Thus, if a man is not capable of putting on and taking off a condom correctly, his mate may need to be taught to do so for him. Should a diaphragm with cream be the contraception chosen for the female, her mate may need to learn to insert the equipment. If the female is on the pill, the man may need to assume responsibility for seeing that she takes it according to schedule.

Contraceptive counseling of special group members must also take into account intellectual and motivational levels. It is known that mentally retarded individuals who are capable of learning other routine tasks are able to learn to utilize appropriate contractive techniques.* However, patient training is essential. Clearly, as with everyone else, the simpler and more foolproof the method the better. At the present time, the I.U.D. is most attractive because when all goes well, there is complete protection after its insertion. But all does not always go well, and back-up abortion may be selected on occasion.

The counselor must also take into account the possibility that the special group member, like other members of his social class, may identify his or her personal status as male or female in part on the basis of fathering or mothering a child. In other words, desire to prove maleness or femaleness may motivate the individual not to use contraception. In some cases, heightened awareness of the responsibilities of parenthood may overcome the notion that parenthood must be achieved. However in cases where the male does not perceive himself as needing to be much involved in child support and rearing, contraception education may have to be focused on the female.

People have often tended to be careless about using contraception because they have felt—"Well, what the hell, if we do get a kid started, we can manage. It wouldn't be fatal." Particularly married couples have been tempted in this way, in part because kids have been expected of them. There are exceptions, but the special group member is far less likely to be able to afford this luxury of whimsical, careless child conceiving. The circumstances of child rearing are likely to be far more difficult for them, be they victims of chronic disease, advancing years, physical or mental handicap. However, as a matter of fact, society is increasingly raising serious questions about careless child conception by anyone.

Question: Should special group members necessarily avoid having children?

----

* Fujita, B.; Wagner, N. N., and Pion, R. J., Sexuality, contraception and the mentally retarded. *Social Medicine*, May 1970.

Answer: This question is dealt with more fully in Chapter 26. Very briefly within the present context, the more useful question may be, is the particular individual up to the task of child care and rearing? Sometimes he or she is. Older persons, legally blind and crippled persons have been known to function very adequately as parents. However, when people face up realistically to the demands of parenthood under the most "normal" circumstances, they are likely to conclude that unless financial wealth is available or a large family-minded group (family or commune) is at hand, the demands of child rearing are likely to be too much for the special group member—just as they frequently are for many other people.

In light of these considerations, contraception education and use would certainly seem to loom large as dimensions of sex education and counseling.

In conclusion. Modern contraception, which is increasingly able to prevent unwanted pregnancy, is ushering in a new era which is helping to make possible new attitudes toward sexual expression. Procreation and sexual recreation may now be viewed as being essentially unrelated. Increasingly, society will question the automatic right to parenthood of just anyone capable of it. But improved contraception is encouraging a "right to sexual expression" attitude for those, including special group members, who wish to claim such a right. Large numbers of members of special groups are interested and are increasingly viewing their potential for sexual enjoyment as a right comparable to the right to basic human needs for survival and health but also for fun, play and other forms of recreation. Parents and professional people, including sex educators and counselors, will undoubtedly need to concern themselves with the question of contraception for members of special groups.

CHAPTER 21

ABORTION

Our state abortion laws, most of which were recently declared unconstitutional by the U.S. Supreme Court, were for the most part established during the last century as a means of protecting women. Many people were practicing medicine without adequate preparation, surgical techniques for this kind of operation were not highly developed and the antibiotics had not yet been discovered—all of which made for exceedingly dangerous induced abortion. As these health hazards were overcome, the ability to have an abortion under medically acceptable conditions became increasingly a matter of financial status. That is, people with money could either obtain a safe abortion here illegally or in a country where it was legal. Less well-off women were forced either to have unwanted children or else to seek illegal abortions in non-hospital, often highly dubious settings.

Today safe abortion is increasingly available to women who want it. Few in this country consider it a method of contraception but rather an indication that contraception has failed.

Question: How does one get an abortion if it is desired?

Answer: Begin by inquiring of one's doctor or health agency. If resistance is encountered at these levels, Planned Parenthood is an excellent source of accurate information which can be contacted either locally or by mail. Of course, the first step to be taken if unwanted pregnancy is suspected is to establish whether it does indeed exist. Laboratory tests can establish this with accuracy within about ten days of conception. In many places, such tests may be conducted without parental consent.

Question: If abortion is going to be done, when is the best time for it?

Answer: As soon as possible after pregnancy is established. Before the fetus is well established in the uterine wall, it may easily and safely be removed by suction techniques requiring no surgery at all, or by simple surgical procedure. Later, minor surgery or chemicals which induce "spontaneous" abortion (e.g., the prostaglandins) are used. Early decision and action are vital to simplicity and safety.

Question: What are the special implications of abortion for members of special groups?

Answer: The question of abortion comes up when doubt is cast upon the wisdom of pregnancy or capacity for child rearing. Some handicapped persons are far better prepared for parenthood than are many other individuals who are simply not temperamentally prepared for child rearing. However, in any case, it should be realized that the demands of child rearing are not only great but also long-term. Members of special groups have functioned extremely well as parents. However, without a great deal of money or extraordinary family support, the task is often especially difficult or even unmanageable for them. Moreover, it may be most difficult to arrange for the adoption of children of special group members. Considering the available alternatives, abortion may be decided upon in the best interests of all concerned.

However, in our tradition women have been under enormous pressure to have children, the worst possible curse being perhaps to be barren. It therefore sometimes happens that even under the worst of conditions, enormous pressure is exerted to avoid termination of pregnancy.

In conclusion. In recent years abortion has been increasingly viewed as a matter to be decided by individual women on the basis of their personal situations and with the consultation of their physicians. This applies also to special group members and helps make feasible examination of the issues and consequences of parenthood on an objective basis. It is certainly true that many members of special groups are perfectly competent to provide adequate child rearing circumstances. Moreover, under certain circumstances such as close family structure and/or wealth or other relatively unusual circumstances, good child rearing conditions are possible even when one or both parents are severely handicapped. For example, severely physically handicapped individuals whose mates are healthy and/or whose other relatives provide ample back-up are very enthusiastic and involved parents. Occasionally the offspring of severely retarded individuals make out quite well because they are not confined to the mentally retarded environment of their parents. In some communal living experiments where everyone's children are considered to be the children of the entire community, individual parents are not required to be up to the herculean task of child rearing by themselves, and the children of members of special groups have virtually the same benefits as all other children. In Russia, communities are established for mentally retarded individuals with the benefit of protective supervision by professionals who are able to relieve the special group members of full responsibility for child rearing.

In other words, abortion, like contraception, provides a means whereby parenthood can be undertaken only when it is desired and circumstances make it a rational choice. For special group members as well as others, abortion makes possible a clear distinction between sex for procreation and sex for recreation and it will probably help to confine the obligations of parenthood to those able and willing to assume them.

CHAPTER 22

CORECREATIONAL ACTIVITIES
AND DATING

CORECREATIONAL, COED OR mixed group activities have long been encouraged among young people, just so they could be labelled "wholesome." "Wholesome" has meant mainly, free of sexual involvement; in other words, carefully supervised. Similarly, for many years, those attempting to help "normalize" the lives of people in various special groups have sought ways of providing or otherwise encouraging corecreational activities for them. Again, the descriptive word "wholesome" has frequently been used to assure that such activities were free of sexual taint. Although all has not always gone as planned, generally speaking corecreational programs have been accepted and valuable parts of the lives of many special groups.

In many countries, dating by young people has traditionally been very carefully controlled, if not discouraged or forbidden. Families and society have simply not wanted to have to deal with the likely consequences of couples being alone for appreciable periods of time. Ironically, while abhorring the likely consequences of unsupervised dating, we have tended to encourage it, even force it on children at an early age. Not at all atypically, a girl became pregnant while baby sitting with her date—while her parents were at a meeting to fight the teaching of contraception in schools.

Unsupervised dating, while very much a part of "normal" growing up in this country, has tended to be perceived as posing a very real threat when sought or engaged in by many special group members. The moral tradition, which defines sexual activity especially and intrinsically bad among special group members has been reenforced by realistic fears of consequences: pregnancy, V.D. and exploitation. If sexual activity out of marriage among certain people is defined as "bad" regardless of consequences, nothing can be done to make it "not bad" except redefinition. On the other hand, something can usually be done about the unacceptable consequences of dating. If consequences of behavior rather than present rules are to determine the morality of behavior, then altering the undesirable consequence of sexual expression would seem to alter its moral status. For example, if sure-fire protection against pregnancy, V.D. and exploitation are provided for selected mental retardates, it may realistically be argued that rules against desired sexual activity in private are groundless.

Question: Under what conditions is unsupervised dating by special group members desirable?

Answer: Whenever the life-enriching possibility of dating is desired by the special group member are not offset by hazards to the individual or others. Many ifs and buts may be implied in this generalization. Individuals relatively sophisticated in such matters prior to illness or injury may need little in the way of counseling or other preparation for dating. Others may benefit from counseling or rap sessions with more experienced peers in everything ranging from how to ask for a date, how to plan it and how to talk with the date. If intercourse is to be involved, there may well need to be coaching in suitable means of intercourse, sex without intercourse, contraception, etc. Older persons may need help with feelings of disloyalty to a deceased mate. Some, such as the inexperienced and the mentally retarded, but not only these groups, may benefit greatly from preparatory practice in the form of role playing if dating is to be successful.

Question: Should sexual activity be considered a part of normal dating behavior among special group members?

Answer: Should it be among dating persons generally? Most parents and teachers probably think not. However, increasing numbers of people seem now to be taking the opposite view and expecting such behavior even among certain special group members. Generalization is therefore not warranted, and individuals and circumstances would seem crucial considerations. Many special group members have tended to be so isolated from members of the complementary sex that a considerable period of time is needed for them to become comfortable enough with them to even consider sexual contacts. For example, many deaf individuals have been so conditioned against matters sexual that in spite of high personal motivation, the interpersonal relationships associated with intimacy may be very difficult for them to develop. Some of our Down's Syndrome children have greatly enjoyed the companionship of a semi-dating situation, physical contact such as hand holding and caressing, but have not seemed interested in genital sex. On the other hand, the common sexual interest associated with dating is evident among special group members such as wheelchair cases, older people and others.

Perhaps the crucial consideration here is the quality of sex education and counseling received by the specific individuals involved. With help and freedom from persecution for having such interest, most members of special groups seem perfectly capable of integrating appropriate sexual behavior into their general dating behavior in ways that do not constitute hazards either to themselves or to society.

In conclusion. There seems little doubt that most individuals are attracted by and are even inspired by well-conducted corecreational programs. As for a further step into single dating, it is likely that because of their earlier life training, societal attitudes of difficulties associated with their problems, many members of special groups will prefer to date without particular interest in making actual sexual contact an aspect of their activities. On the other hand, it seems more than likely that increasing numbers of such individuals are going to see the circumstances of dating as leading quite naturally to some form of sexual expression. Without imposing the desires of one group upon the other, educators and counselors will undoubtedly feel increased obligation to help special group members do what they choose to do with all of the appropriate knowledge and skills and psychological preparation that can be made available. Sensitivity to individual needs and interests is of course of crucial importance here, for stereotypes associated with special group classification may have little or no meaning for particular individuals.

At any rate, dating among special group members, whether or not it entails direct sexual elements, certainly provides one of the more attractive recreational resources for members of special groups. If available resources are utilized, it need not necessarily be avoided or rendered overly restricted because of fears of sexual involvement. Consequently, as education and counseling in this area improve, it is to be expected that increasing numbers of members of special groups will avail themselves of their sexual resources for enjoyable living, including while dating.

CHAPTER 23

SEXUAL INADEQUACY

E VERY ESTIMATE SUGGESTS that there are large numbers of people, perhaps more than fifty percent of married couples, who suffer from some form of sexual inadequacy which prevents sexual intercourse from being the fulfilling experience that is sought. Sexual inadequacy in the male is often termed "impotence." It refers to the inability to have or maintain an erection as desired. It may also refer to the "premature" ejaculation, the inability to withhold ejaculation until the desired time. In females it refers to the inability to reach full and satisfying climax. (The term "frigidity" has been used to cover such a range of difficulties ranging from lack of feeling, refusal of the vagina to open, refusal to respond to a particular would-be lover, pain in intercourse, etc., that it is not a very useful word for identifying a particular condition.)

Although medical conditions may account for such problems of dysfunction, by and large, and particularly with regard to males, the difficulty is more likely to be due to psychological factors. In the absence of actual data on this subject, it would probably be reasonable to suppose that the incidence of inadequacy is at least as high among members of special groups. In some such groups the incidence may be even higher due to specific handicapping conditions and societal attitudes. Only in recent years have professional people begun to take such problems of sexual dysfunction seriously and to learn how to treat them. There is now the tendency to classify them along with other problems of bodily dysfunction or psychosocial adjustment, and to approach them as being "curable" in most cases. Perhaps the most important development in this regard is the increasing tendency of people to view such problems as sexual inadequacy as they would a tooth problem, a vision problem or a digestion problem, that is, as legitimate human problems for which professional help may comfortably be sought. In past years it usually did not cross people's minds that professional help might be useful to them. If they did seek such help, it was with herculean effort. And, generally speaking, the professional approached was unprepared by training to be useful. Increasingly however, people are feeling free to come quickly to the point of their difficulty, to describe it and to ask what might be done about it. Increasingly, too, professional people are being trained to provide such help.

Question: What are the causes of sexual inadequacy?

Answer: Physical causes in the male may include various disease conditions such as some cases of diabetes (certainly some diabetics are very active sexually), excessive drinking and aging. In the female, physical causes may range all the way from absence of a vagina or refusal of a vagina to open sufficiently for penis entry ("vaginismus"), to restrictions of clitoris response and structural problems which may give rise to pain rather than pleasure. Some hormonal and even allergic reactions may give rise to inability to respond sexually. In other words, when problems in this area are to be treated, it is wise to begin with medical evaluation to rule out or treat organic problems. As a matter of fact, in medical sex clinics such as that of Masters and Johnson treatment of sexual inadequacy in both the male and female begins with a thorough physical examination. Particularly in females, medical conditions may exist which cannot be alleviated by any amount of counseling or psychotherapy.

However, the most likely cause of sexual dysfunctioning in both the male and the female is psychological in nature and/or based on communication disorders. For example, the antisexual conditioning from early childhood of a great many females has rendered them incapable of the kind of relaxed abandon that may be necessary for them to reach climax; they may be incapable of the easy talking out and reeducation they need because they have been convinced the whole subject is unspeakable. Their reeducation may entail having to learn to enjoy basic body communication such as physical contact, caressing, gentle stimulation of all potential erotic zones of the body and genital play. Intensive anti-masturbatory training may have deprived the individual of a feeling of freedom to explore her own sexual parts. Sexual play and its culmination in orgasm may never have been learned. Intensive professional help may be needed to release the individual from her masturbatory and mutual stimulation revulsion if sexual fulfillment is to be discovered. The same kinds of problems may occur among males. However, their inadequacy is more likely to be based on ignorance of female sexual responses and preoccupation with whether or not they are living up to their notions of manliness.

Question: Since successful sexual functioning has obviously been so important for human survival, why is it that so many people have serious problems?

Answer: In the first place, many people are born with or develop structural or physiological sex problems, just as many are born with or develop visual or coordination problems. Some of these are readily correctable but others are not. For example, numerous women who experience painful intercourse (dyspareunia) have medically correctable adhesions between clitoris and prepuce (clitoris hood). On the other hand, some men have such small penises that vaginal penetration is not possible; and some males and females have neural or hormonal problems which virtually eliminate hope of adequate sexual functioning.

In the vast majority of cases, however, sexual disorders in male and female are due to antisexual child-rearing practices and other psychological factors. Even adhesions between prepuce and clitoris or prepuce and glans penis may be due to the infant's having been prevented from doing the normal exploring or tugging at his or her genitals. Moreover, it is to be expected that children trained to consider their genitals and sexual impulses bad or dirty will find it difficult to adjust suddenly and comfortably to sexual involvement with another. Many such negatively trained individuals cannot masturbate successfully. Other psychological factors which undermine sexual adequacy include the traditional language barrier which prevents easy communication about sexual matters even between loving mates. Then there is the preoccupation, especially perhaps among males, with being a great sexual performer rather than merely an enjoyer of sex. (After all, if you can't open your mouth in a meeting unless you have something absolutely brilliant to say, you will not likely speak up very often or very easily or very usefully—because you're too preoccupied with being brilliant.)

The intermixing of and conflicts among possible physical and psychological aspects of sexual inadequacy are illustrated by the following case. A promising candidate for military flight training was distinguished among his fellows as being the most "horny" in a sexually preoccupied and eager group. However, he was dropped from the program when medical evaluated revealed his penis and testicles to be in an extreme state of atrophy. There was evidently no biological basis for his sexual hyperenthusiasm but his need to demonstrate masculinity made him behave as though "abnormally driven sexually." Of course, no counseling was available to help him adjust to the realities of his situation.

Question: What can be done about psychological based inadequacy?

Answer: Of course, this is too large a question to be treated here fully. However, following are some important considerations.

Psychoanalytic treatment has been abandoned by more and more sexologists and sex therapists in recent years because it is likely to be too time consuming (many years), too costly and too likely to fail. Faster, more effective approaches do not attempt to dig back to childhood traumas for insight. Rather, they attack as directly as possible problems and symtpoms as they exist now. For example, treatment of vaginismus (an involuntary contracting of the muscles of the vaginal opening which makes penis entry impossible or very difficult and painful) may begin by encouraging the enjoyment of sex without intercourse, i.e., especially by hand, mouth or vibrator. Some couples find sex without intercourse entirely satisfactory and may not be concerned with treatment of the vaginismus. In such circumstances, the condition may treat itself, in that underlying fears of penetration resulting in muscular tension may be eased by sexual enjoyment without intercourse. If not, a happy sexual relationship may thus be maintained while the vaginismus itself is systematically treated by attitudinal change and gradual training in vaginal receptiveness.

Treatment of impotency in the male may also begin by teaching him to give and receive enjoyment without vaginal penetration. Treatment may be as simple as correcting body discomfort or positioning during coition, supplementing lubrication, reducing alcoholic consumption prior to sex, having sex when not so fatigued or improving physical fitness. Very commonly, the "impotent" male is defeating himself by worrying about how well he is performing according to some criterion he has picked up either from the usual sources or even from well-meaning sex manuals. His treatment may best be in terms of learning to perceive intercourse not as a proving ground, but as a relaxed, fun occasion when the only criteria of success are giving and receiving pleasure by whatever means.

Either partner may, quite unintentionally, be demoralizing the other and perhaps himself, by one or more of several means, including:

1. putting down the partner's (or their own) efforts by sarcastic remarks, derisive laughter or odious comparisons. (Every fairly intelligent prostitute—or golf pro—

knows that you bring customers back not by ridiculing performance but by complimenting it and holding up bright prospects for the future.)

2. rigidly insisting that there is one right or optimal means of intercourse and that other means are inadequate if not indecent or immoral.

3. refusing to take initiative in "turning on" an inexperienced, worried or distracted partner. The male who does not immediately present an eager erection may respond readily to gentle "attack" upon his penis by mouth and/or lubricated hands. The "unready" female may soon respond to body stroking, finger and mouth techniques, careful use of a vibrator or other activity. Incidentally, "turning on" another person is an almost surefire way of arousing oneself.

With or without professional help, sometimes with only the help of good sex manuals or simple counseling, most individuals suffering from sexual dysfunction can probably undergo therapeutic reeducation. That is, they may come to realize that sexuality is as much a natural part of them as their appetite for food and their enjoyment of other forms of play. They may overcome their reluctance to touch and stimulate their genitals and learn to relax and enjoy this without guilt feelings. They may learn to experiment with themselves and a partner to discover just what forms of stimulation are likely to bring about sexual enjoyment, maximal arousal and orgasmic release.

In the so-called sex clinics, an effort is made to tie theory with practice. That is, couples are at first dealt with on a verbal level then taught to put their new understandings into practice together. Similarly, the marriage counselor is likely to explore the client's inhibitions and other problems in the office but to give the client homework to do, which may include masturbating with the aid of a suitable lubricant and in the case of the female, with the aid of an electrical vibrator, gentle jet of warm water or other mechanical device which is likely to encourage sexual arousal. Erotic pictures or anything else that the counselor determines as sexually stimulating for the client are likely to be recommended in such a training program. If a mate is not available who will work with the unresponsive individual, a sexual companion may be needed who can help overcome resistance to sexual responsiveness. Some clinics require that clients bring a partner with them. Others undertake to provide paid and trained sexual companions.

Question: Does the problem of sexual dysfunction have special implications for members of special groups?

Answer: Yes, very probably. As common as problems of sexual dysfunction are in the population at large, the incidence is undoubtedly even greater among many special group members. Society at large has traditionally been at war with sex, and this has been even more true with regard to special groups. The impact of this attitude undoubtedly affects sexual functioning. For example, those labelled mentally retarded are likely to approach any new situation with low confidence levels and high expectations of failure, both of which could easily reduce prospects of success, including in sexual undertakings. The situation is similar with older people who are not "supposed" to be sexual and who are likely to have grave doubts as to their ability to function adequately, particularly if they have some health problem. Individuals with deformities or orthopedic difficulties may face unique problems. In addition, the special group member is very likely to have more or less concern over the question of how he is affecting his mate.

If people generally need a great deal of help in learning to accept themselves as worthwhile human beings, to accept their fallibility and right to make mistakes, to accept and even cherish their sexual selves as any other potential that they might wish to cultivate, members of special groups are even more in need of assistance in this area.

Therefore, it might be said that the first problem in the sex education and counseling of special groups members is to overcome the traditional teachings and training of the population at large and then to attack whatever specific problems are generated by the circumstances which make special group members special. For example, some individuals have succeeded in overcoming traditional attitudes toward prostitution in order to make such visits possible for mentally retarded boys. Then the prostitutes have had to be trained so as to make the experience "successful" for the particular individual rather than yet another inroad into his feelings of adequacy and self-worth.

In conclusion. Most sexual dysfunction is learned and so of course can be unlearned and replaced with behavior likely to give rise to satisfacotry sexual functioning. The first step in any effort to overcome sexual dysfunctioning is to eliminate possible medical sources of the difficulty, particularly true with respect to females. Medical problems aside, education and counseling are now able to overcome most problems of dysfunction. Such education and counseling, if desired, should be sought as readily as comparable help for other treatable conditions such as visual, dental or foot problems about which people typically feel free to seek help. But the learner and teacher or counselor may need to be even more objective and bold than usual because the usual problems may be exaggerated by special problems of special group members. However, increasing numbers of people will undoubtedly rise to this kind of occasion to help the special group member achieve or at least partially achieve the kind of sex life important to him. We will never know the numbers of parents and friends who have overcome their own prejudices and reluctance in order to help special group members overcome obstacles to sexual fulfillment. In the future there will undoubtedly be more openness and respectability in providing such help as it is needed.

CHAPTER 24

PAID SEXUAL COMPANIONS

In the course of history, paid sexual companions (prostitutes) have been utilized by men but also by women to meet what are considered sexual needs. At some times and places prostitution has been viewed as a respected profession, and even, in early times, as a religious obligation. In our tradition, however, it has tended to be viewed in darkest colors unless performed in a self-sacrificing way in the interests of loved ones. Today, prostitution thrives for various reasons: it is a sure way of removing doubts as to the inclusion of sex in a liaison or date; it provides a desired service that is perhaps not otherwise available; it absolves one of any feeling of need to become emotionally involved; and it provides for pleasures that a legal mate may be unable or unwilling to provide. In recent years, paid sexual companions have even been used to a considerable extent in scientific sex research and in the treatment of problems of sexual inadequacy.

In some cases members of special groups are married to individuals with whom they are sexually compatible and who will make every effort to accomplish a happy sexual adjustment. However, marriage is not necessarily a panacea. For example, incapacities or special problems of the special group member may require that the husband or wife accept and learn sexual techniques which might previously not have been considered acceptable or may even have been considered unnatural or perverse acts. Moreover, a husband or wife may not be able, at least without intensive counseling, to accept the altered physical, verbal or psychological changes in the special group member and may literally be revolted at the idea of sexual contact with him or her. Although some wives of war-injured men have been not only willing but anxious to make whatever adjustments might be necessary in the interest of a happy sexual life, others have simply not been able to perceive the wounded individual as being the same person and sexual partner he had been. The ravages of disease in either sex may produce similar problems.

In addition to the sex-related problems which may exist within marriage, there are the numerous problems associated with those unmarried individuals having all the sexual interests and inclinations of the most happily married. Such individuals may find considerable relief in masturbation by hand or with the use of various devices, and still others are in position to cultivate homosexual contacts which are not only sexually gratifying but may have amative or loving aspects for them which greatly enhance the experience.

The fact remains, however, that heterosexual enjoyment is of the essence for the great majority of individuals, including special group members. There is, therefore, the problem of gratifying such desires among those individuals who are not married and who are not able to find auto-eroticism or homosexuality available or adequate substitutes for what they consider to be the real thing. For example, war-injured individuals are frequently not married or, if they are, they do not have ready access to their mates but still attach the highest importance not only to sexual gratification itself but also to demonstrating the continued capability for sexual response and competence. In these and many other situations, the question is then posed, "Where are suitable sexual partners to be found—partners who will function with the individual regardless of age, disability or appearance?"

Moral considerations simply eliminate exploring such a question at all for a great many people, be they special group members or those responsible for them. On the other hand, there is the perhaps growing attitude that anything which harmlessly enhances the life of the special group member, including any available form of sexual outlet, is entirely legitimate. In other words, there is the philosophy that the special group member's lot in life is difficult enough without unnecessarily adding deprivations such as enforced sexual abstinence.

For those capable of considering it, prostitution provides an opportunity for gratifying sexual outlet for a great many members of special groups. Since the words "prostitution" and "prostitute" have traditionally been dirty words, more acceptable terms have been proposed which convey the idea of providing a useful or even therapeutic service. For example, the terms "paid sexual companion," "surrogate lover" and "medical courtesan" have all been used to convey the desired meaning while perhaps minimizing moral issues.

One very large group of special group members is composed of individuals or couples who suffer from psychologically based sexual inadequacy. Sex clinics, modeled after the Masters and Johnson clinic, require that such individuals be treated as couples, which is to say that either husband or wife must undergo treatment together or a surrogate lover must be utilized. In some such programs, paid sexual companions have been provided routinely for the benefit of those patients either lacking a mate or having a mate unwilling to participate in this form of therapy. Some of the sex clinics emerging in recent years have all but institutionalized the idea that a special kind of prostitute may have an important role to play in meeting the needs of special group members.

In addition, it is important to realize that for many years therapists of various kinds, including psychotherapists and gynecologists, have sometimes utilized the services of selected prostitutes as an aspect of their therapeutic program with some patients. For example, some individuals endeavoring to break away from homosexual orientation have been referred by therapists to prostitutes who have been carefully coached to help the patient overcome such things as fear of women and other heterosexual hang-ups.

Question: Have prostitutes actually been used routinely for the benefit of special group members?

Answer: Yes, but to an unkown extent. For example, for many years many psychotherapists have referred patients or clients to prostitutes whom they have known and trusted as an aspect of their therapy—just as other doctors might refer patients to physical therapists or other individuals for supportive therapy. Some of the sex clinics which insist upon treating couples rather than individuals provide paid sexual companions for those individuals who do not present themselves with a mate for treatment. And over the years, there is no way of knowing how many sympathetic parents or guardians have sought out paid sexual companions for the handicapped person in their care. It is probably safe to assume that "male necessity" has brought males the advantage of such companionship to a far greater extent than females, even though the female interest might have been equally great. An exception to this generalization is that special group composed of middle-aged well-to-do females, usually, single, who can hire a male sexual companion for sexual therapy or beach boys or escorts when on vacation.

The only organized and frankly reported use of prostitutes for the benefit of certain special group members that has come to my attention is that of Eloisa de Lorenzo at a school for the mentally retarded in Montevido, Uruguay. Lorenzo, an internationally renowned leader in the mental retardation field, recognizing the emotional and sexual make-up and needs of the mentally retarded, began in the 1930's to coach girls with respect to their bodily changes and menstruation, the appropriate expression of affection, and so forth. This approach seemed to work very well with the girls who also had the benefit of close supervision of mothers and sisters, but the boys were another matter. Their masturbatory behavior was considered both excessive and not well regulated by awareness of time and place. Then a crisis developed when homosexuals sought them out.

The boys would not discuss the matter with the teachers or doctors at the school but, significantly, they would confide in the school's carpenter and gardener. These men discovered that the boys were having sexual relations with other males mostly because of their fear of having sexual relations with women. "They didn't know how to relate to women. They felt very inadequate." Upon discovering this, the teachers set about finding prostitutes with health certificates who would accept coaching with regard to introducing the young men to the practice of intercourse under the guidance of a mature woman who wouldn't laugh at them and who would treat them in a manner discussed in advance. Doctors helped select specific prostitutes who came to the school and discussed the entire situation with the teachers. The parents of the boys were then advised of the plan; all were surprised to find that the parents were grateful for being included in the experiment, for they were afraid of developing homosexuality or of unsupervised visits to brothels with all the disease, exploitation, mishaps and ridicule this might mean.

The parents of the boys granted written permission for the boys' participation. The boys were all over twenty years of age and had IQ's between fifty and about sixty-five. The prostitutes quickly appreciated the importance of the role expected of them in terms of functioning as companions and teachers, and they declined to charge for their services. Some of the boys went to the prostitutes many times; others did not. "When they came back they were so proud and they told the teacher: 'Now, I am a man, I don't need it any more. Now I know what it's all about.' " When they wanted to return they were merely asked to be sure to go with a companion and to confine themselves to the designated girls.

This program went on for the three remaining years while Mrs. Lorenzo was principal of that school. She commented that at the time she had sons of her own and very much hoped that when sexual matters would become of great importance to them as they grew older they would have the benefit of such open-minded and warm-hearted guidance as the school boys had had. For their part, the prostitutes wrote letters and otherwise reported what a wonderful opportunity the plan had been for them to provide a worthwhile service. One reported on a young man's "defect" which had previously not been noticed. The program ended when Mrs. Lorenzo left the school.[1]

Question: What about such a program for girls and women?

Answer: There is no way of knowing how many such programs have been established and quietly conducted for male members of special groups in the course of history. If such programs would be expected to run into opposition when set up for males, certainly opposition would be even stronger if proposed for females. Masters and Johnson declined to provide such service for women as they originally did for men. Thomas Durkin, head of the North Berkeley Counseling Center, openly provides carefully coached sex surrogates for women in sex therapy. If such a service should become established for men, there seems little doubt that the new assertiveness of women will demand like-treatment for females.

Question: What about the matter of training or coaching of the paid sexual companion?

Answer: This is certainly a matter of greatest importance if this kind of service is to be useful. People in general and many members of special groups in particular have had very little introduction to the realities of sex and they are likely to have little preparation for abrupt confrontation with it. They are prone to be very vulnerable.

For this reason, therapists who use prostitutes as adjunctive therapy select the prostitute with great care and devote considerable time to coaching her so that her influence will be constructive rather than destructive—which it might otherwise very well be. For example, an unfeeling, untrained prostitute might very well laugh at, ridicule or express revulsion toward a person seeking recreational sex or some sort of therapy. Such behavior could be thoroughly demoralizing.

---

[1] Molly C. Gorelick, "A Simple Course in Sex," *Human Behavior* (March, 1973).

Question: Do you anticipate the increased use of paid sexual companions for members of special groups?

Answer: Yes. People are finding it increasingly possible to seek out those sexual experiences they consider important, and society continues to frown but not so maliciously as before. In fact, these days people seem to be expected to work out their own life styles, including sex, pretty much on their own. A somewhat different psychology seems to apply with regard to many members of special groups, although it is true that special group members are less likely to be considered "less than human" in their emotional and sexual makeup than used to be the case. Moreover, there seems to be a growing recognition that frequently special group members are more restricted with regard to potential satisfactions in life and, therefore, available satisfactions should not arbitrarily be denied them. The more "pathetic" the condition of the special group member, the more likely society is to grant him little pleasures without too much protest, as in the case of the war-injured paraplegics and quadraplegics.

Thus, it is even possible to imagine the emergence of respected, paid, sexual companion specialists devoted to the service of various special groups.

CHAPTER 25

MARRIAGE BY SPECIAL GROUP MEMBERS

As a general statement, divorce statistics and studies indicate that marriage tends to be precarious relationship which, while highly prized by some, can barely be tolerated or not tolerated at all by others. Like other people, special group members often marry without any real awareness of what they are getting into, and do not find the new adjustment demands acceptable. Also, like others, they may view marriage as a substitute for personal therapy ("someone to watch over me . . ."); and soon be dis-illusioned to find the mate lacking in the professional qualifications they seek. Or worse still, the mate may be expecting some-one to watch over him! On the other hand, special group members may find in marriage the opportunity of a lifetime for a close relationship, cooperative undertakings, understanding and worth-while communication.

State laws concerned with prohibiting marriage have the intent of preventing the creation of a marital contract "when one of the partners is incapable of understanding the nature of the relationships and preventing reproduction by persons whose issue may become a public charge."[1] Persons considered not capable of marriage are described in a wide variety of terms including "idiots, insane, weak-minded, lunatics, feeble-minded, imbeciles, persons incapable of contracting and persons of un-sound mind." Persons so judged are considered unable to under-stand the nature of the marriage relation and the duties and

---

[1] *The Mentally Disabled and the Law*, Samuel J. Brakel and Ronald S. Rock, eds., Revised ed. (Chicago: The University of Chicago Press, 1971).

obligations involved. The eugenic argument reduces to the question of whether the mentally disabled person is fit for parenthood. This test of competency for parenthood reflects the traditional view that marriage necessarily implies having children, which is not the case, especially since the contraception revolution.

With regard to enforcement of prohibitions against marrying, the status is questionable. Only twenty states have attempted to establish any machinery to enforce the prohibitions; eighteen states provide criminal punishments for violations. Penalties vary from minor fines to a maximum of five years' imprisonment. The punitive measures apply usually to the incompetent person, often also to the clerk or official granting the marriage license, and in a few states also to anyone "advising," "abetting" or "causing" the marriage. North Carolina, North Dakota and Oregon require that a medical certificate avowing the absence of the prohibited conditions be produced before any marriage license can be issued.

Kansas requires the county clerk to ask the applicants if they have ever been legally judged "an incapacitated person" and, if so, whether they have been discharged or restored. In the absence of specific statutory instructions, clerks can hardly be expected to ask such questions. One Texas clerk, queried on the point, reportedly replied, "Are you serious? How can I ask a person if he is crazy?" It has been concluded that the statutes preventing marriage of people with mental disabilities have in fact prevented very few such marriages and have "thus far invariably proved worthless, chiefly because of the lack of adequate provision for the identification or diagnosis of the mental status of applicants for marriage licenses." At least twelve states no longer judge epileptics mental incompetents forbidden to marry. Physical disabilities, no matter how severe (e.g., quadraplegia), do not disqualify persons for either marriage or parenthood.

Legal restrictions aside, members of special groups, like all others, view marriage as a "right" to which they are entitled. In fact, some special group members have found marriage especially gratifying, particularly after years of loneliness or after the loss of close companionship to which they had become thoroughly accustomed. Certainly individuals with similar handicaps or conditions might be expected to be particularly sympathetic toward each other's interests, needs and anxieties, and may find in such mutual understanding enhanced relationships. Mattinson's study of the marriages of thirty-two couples where both parties were mentally handicapped and both had been patients at a mental hospital for short or long periods indicated generally good marital adjustment and happiness among the couples involved. One important factor in marital success was that the individuals viewed it as a challenge which obligated them to make a "go" of the relationship. According to the criteria set by the author, the couples may be said to have made out reasonably well, with husbands and wives complementing each other in terms of their respective abilities. For example, it was not surprising that one of the people was usually much more verbal than the other and was therefore able to serve as interpreter for his or her mate and increase the effectiveness of their communications with others. They married for pretty much the usual reasons, ranging from deciding to give it a try after a long or short courtship, usually in the institution, to having to marry because of pregnancy. Usually their expectations of success in marriage were low to begin with and those who made out reasonably well were especially gratified and probably motivated to continue the "successful" performance. Generally speaking, they continued to look after themselves and perhaps their children in ways considered acceptable to the communities in which they lived.[2]

On the other hand, there has also been a tendency to glorify marriage for special group members as though it were a panacea which might if not resolve existing problems, at least provide a refuge from life's stresses and demands. In other words, special group members, like people generally, have frequently viewed marriage as an easy solution to personal problems which are merely aggravated by the very special demands made by marriage

---

[2] Janet Mattinson, *Marriage and Mental Handicap* (Pittsburgh: University of Pittsburgh Press, 1970).

—particularly if it is complicated by children. The euphoria of the courtship period, which encourages feelings of easy and perhaps profound communication between people, does not necessarily carry over for any considerable period of time into marriage. Thus marriage may be followed by disillusionments and bitterness engendered in part by the very things which made the courtship so attractive. One deaf couple married because of the fun and adventure they had experienced together during their leisure hours, soon recognized profound differences in preferred life styles and attitudes towards sexual activity. They had two children in the usual effort toward marriage therapy, with the idea that the children would surely reunite them with a common interest. For the sake of the children, they maintained a home together, but insofar as possible lived their separate lives and by long-standing mutual agreement separated the moment the younger boy finished college. In contrast, a blind couple, both of whom had felt rejected by others in their previous lives, continued to find each other the most rewarding company they have ever known. A married quadraplegic and paraplegic who had two children of their own continued to find each other unbelievably lucky finds because of their uniquely shared interests, including the erotic.

Question: What general statements might be made about marriage on the part of special group members?

Answer: At least two, and these probably apply equally to marriages in general. There is a tremendous need for starkly realistic education and counseling for marriage and a continuation of such education and counseling during marriage, particularly perhaps during its early stages and at times of crisis.* Historically, the functions of marriage have been quite clear-cut. Man and wife have had definite, mutually supporting roles to play and children to rear. Children were usually viewed as crucial, namely as workers, sickness insurance and old age insurance. Today, these functions

---

* For example see Mace, D., *Sexual Difficulties in Marriage.* Philadelphia, Fortress Press, 1972.

of marriage have been lost to a considerable extent; couples often need professional guidance to help them determine just what marriage means to them personally.

As with other people, some special group members find it valuable to experience a period of trial marriage so as to determine whether the compatability of playing together can extend into the more routine and stressful aspects of actually living together. In some cases this approach has worked out nicely, in part because parents and society generally have sometimes been prone to be especially lenient toward this kind of thing among handicapped persons. On the other hand, such experimentation with marriage would be entirely unacceptable to individuals or couples whose training has emphasized learning to adjust wholeheartedly to the accepted standards of their society. Counseling may be especially valuable at this point in helping individuals to ascertain just what approach is likely to be best for them personally.

Question: Generally speaking, what is the attitude of professional people toward the marriage of special group members?

Answer: Insofar as I can tell, it is generally favorable, particularly when viewed as an option to be considered and when it gives promise of being a mutually supportive relationship. As with the advisability of having children, the matter of marriage needs to be viewed on such an individual basis that individual cases rather than sweeping generalizations would be in order.

In conclusion. Marriage may contribute greatly to the quality of life of many members of special groups and may add to their feeling of belonging to and functioning within their society at large. It may also lead to embitterment and feelings of greater distance and isolation if members are not prepared for the realities of intimate living and working together. In other words, marriage may be an incomparable boon or it may be a real bust—

just as it may among people at large. Education and counseling in this entire area has been woefully lacking, both with respect to the special group member himself and with respect to society at large.

PARENTHOOD BY SPECIAL
GROUP MEMBERS

C ONSIDERATION OF THIS subject might best begin with the broader consideration of the general meaning of parenthood. If people were forewarned in a realistic manner about what is involved in bearing, rearing and educating children and in meeting the child's needs, large numbers who are uncertain anyway would undoubtedly question the wisdom of such a large commitment of themselves, their time, their interests and their money. A few brief examples may make my meaning perfectly clear.

First, there is the mundane question of expense. Child rearing is extremely expensive, and if parents aspire to a college education for their children, they must think of an expenditure in excess of $50,000 at the very least. If they take into account the likely inability of the mother to bring in wages during the growing-up period, this amount may exceed $100,000. Since parenthood, with its demands, inconveniences, costs and sacrificing of personal interests is not considered by most a highly pleasurable experience, the question might well be raised, "Is this really the way I want to spend such a large proportion of my income, time and energy?"

The second consideration is the characteristics of children. Children are not always little bundles of joy that fit nicely into the family pattern. On the contrary, in addition to the usual diseases, teething and other situations that rob parents of their sleep, children go through normal developmental stages during which they sometimes seem pitted against the parents' happiness and well being. Indeed, the behavior of the normal child at some time reflects signs of many types of psychopathology from phobic reactions to manic-depression states, schizophrenic hallucinating, obsessions, compulsions, sociopathic behaviors and a devotion to making a mess, preferably with such material as their feces. For example, they might get a high fever in the evening, keep mother up all night and be bright and eager to go the next morning while mother faces another grim day without benefit of rest. Training for parenthood rarely includes confrontation with these realities.

The third consideration is the characteirstics of the child-rearing environment. Stated very briefly, this is not a children's world. It is unbelievably unadjusted to their developmental needs. There are such simple matters as the fact that the furniture does not fit them. Moreover, as most adults are sedentary, the environment is designed for sitters and spectators. Children live in a movement world. Not only do most homes discourage movement, but well-designed, well-maintained convenient play facilities are rare indeed. Children, therefore, tend to be highly frustrated in their natural quest for movement, adventure and exploration and are forced to find activity in forbidden places, such as busy streets. The great majority are incarcerated in schools for large blocks of time where the chief virtues continue to be sitting quietly and being still. And, lastly, automobiles have rendered the environment almost unbelievably dangerous for children, in addition to rendering much of the best of it inaccessible for children's play and other activities.

These considerations would seem to make it perfectly clear that the situation provides many obstacles to reasonably comfortable child rearing even though the particular child might be as well adjusted and conforming as anyone might ask. How about children with special problems? Parents of children with special problems have similar, but more serious situations to deal with than other parents. Their children are likely to be vastly more expensive to look after, much more demanding of time and less able to cope with the existing anti-child environment than other children.

In brief, I have concluded that an honest parenthood education would lead most people to consider very carefully whether or not to have children, that, is unless they were well prepared by training, were very rich and could afford supplemental assistance or could bring the children up within a large family context in which all labors could be shared with close and loving relatives. The only alternative if parenthood is to be made a reasonable undertaking would be for prospective parents to insist upon fundamental improvements in the circumstances of child rearing which would involve a major series of readjustments in community planning, design and resources.

Having children under present circumstances is a most difficult undertaking, particularly for the mother. It is likely to damage the relationship between husband and wife, to force all manner of adjustments in life style and to lack much in the way of compensating rewards—and this is assuming that the children are "normal" in the sense of not being special group members and being capable of conforming to the usual developmental and educational expectancies. If the children do have special developmental problems, then the situation is bound to be worse on all counts, the cost being higher (perhaps astronomically so), the demands on time and energy greater and the selection of a developmentally appropriate environment and educational setting for the child all the more difficult.

This is the context within which the question whether it is desirable for members of special groups to have children should be raised. I personally am convinced that the majority of people are unprepared by realistic training for parenthood, that the deck is stacked against this being a particularly happy or successful undertaking for most parents and that special group members with their generaly more liimted resources are likely to find the demands of parenthood particularly difficult, if not impossible.

Question: Is it your contention then that special group members ought never to undertake parenthood?

Answer: Not necessarly. The question is not really whether or not the prospective parent is a special group member. The question is whether the particular individual or couple is prepared to deal reasonably successfully with parenthood. For reasons of temperament, training and interest, a great many "normal" individuals are not prepared or qualified for or interested in becoming parents and only do so from a feeling of obligation or from carelessness.

On the other hand, if reasonably well-to-do, well-educated and well-supported members of special groups (including older people, blind and paraplegic individuals) seriously desire children and understand reasonably well what is involved in child rearing, they are sometimes able to do a perfectly adequate job by any of the usual standards. Of course, such groups as the mentally retarded are particularly hard pressed to prepare their children for successful adjustment and performance in our very complex and competitive society even though their children might be entirely normal intellectually. Mentally retarded parents are likely to be able to provide only a limited intellectual environment for their children and thereby place them at a distinct disadvantage.

The basic point here is not to render a decision as to whether or not members of special groups "should" attempt parenthood. Rather, the point is that except for the quite wealthy and for those few who exist within the context of a large, closely knit family, under present circumstances parenthood and child rearing are most impressively difficult undertakings at best. If, however, the children have any of the health or developmental problems which are so common, or if they do not fit neatly into the usual community including school programs, then the problems of child rearing are enormously magnified. Families whose children are even a little slow in learning how to tie their shoes, left from right, how to read or write, and other tasks by a certain age are often traumatized because of the child's inability to "keep up." Of course, really serious problems frequently have a devastating effect upon family dynamics even in those situations where the parents are highly educated and financially well off. Mothers in particular tend to be blamed for children's problems and to feel the impact of the usual attitude that if only they did their job a little more adequately, the child's difficulty would vanish or would not have occurred in the first place.

So, the question reduces to something like this: If, under present circumstances, parenthood really poses such an extraordinarily difficult challenge for non-special group members, what kind of challenge or problem is it likely to pose for special group members? It seems a shame that so many people, including so many special group members, feel the need to have childern, not because of the intrinsic attractiveness of child bearing but because of self-defeating needs to prove masculinity or femininity or because of the truly grotesque notion that children will magically bring them the happiness, perhaps even mental therapy and meaning in life that they seek.

In conclusion. Parenthood is a most difficult undertaking, and decisions concerning whether or not to attempt it would seem to invite the most careful of anticipatory education and counseling, for special group members even more than for others.

IN CONCLUSION

THE REMARKABLE ACHIEVEMENTS of special education during
the past quarter century should not blind us to a significant
failure of those who would serve special groups. These people
have generally failed to confront educationally a most prominent
factor in personality functioning: sexuality. This book represents
an admittedly ambitious effort to do something constructive
about this failure.

As noted eariler, reasons for the failure derive from several
sources, including the sex conflicted nature of our society which
results in our being both sex-centric and sex-rejecting;[1] the
prevalence of our misconceptions about sex accompanied by our
general ignorance of the subject; our uncertainty as to just what
constitutes a good sex education program for people generally,
let alone special groups; our conflicted but in important ways
negative attitudes toward special groups; our misperception of
the sexuality of special group members; and our mistaken notion
that the special group member's label necessarily tells us something useful about his sexuality.

Part I of this book has attempted to put into perspective
some of the foregoing sources of our failure to provide worthwhile
sex education and counseling for special groups. Moreover, a
critical view of the concept of "normality" reveals that the word
makes for great confusion because it can have at least five
legitimate meanings, ranging from the moral to the statistical.
Three possible philosophies of sex education and counseling for
special groups are noted—to eliminate sexual interest, to tolerate
it or to cultivate it. Some precautions are suggested with regard
to providing sex education and counseling. These precautions are
mainly to avoid giving the impression that special group members

---

[1] Johnson and Belzer, *op. cit.*, Chapter 3.

necessarily are or should be deeply sensuous or in need of help with sexual matters.

Part II has included discussion of sexual developmental events and related matters of special concern to parents and others working with individuals of all ages in special groups. Topics have been discussed in general terms, common questions concerning them asked and answered, and relevant special applications made to special groups. Of course, every effort has been made to reflect the best of modern knowledge on these subjects. However, there is room for modesty as to what we really know in some areas. Some of the material, being straightforward and objective, may be at odds with popular notions concerning, for example, pornography, nudity and prostitution. However, a first step toward rationality in this area is to equip oneself with the best available facts. Accurate knowledge often destroys troublesome bugaboos which have led to all manner of irrational even damaging behavior and suffering—for example, the mistaken notion that masturbation damages physical and mental health.

The intent of this book is to serve special groups and those who would serve them, but also to raise questions about the usefulness of the concept of "special" groups. Clearly there is merit in identifying the specialness of certain groups and individuals if they are to receive their fair treatment as human beings and not be relegated to some inferior, neglected status. However, if we insist upon placing people in categories, we find that everyone is in at least one if not several special groups. It is very special to be male or female, sexually speaking. It is special to be a child, a young adult, a married or unmarried adult, a mother or father, a childless married person, a divorced or elderly person, an athlete, a non-athlete, wealthy or poor, a conservative Christian, a non-Christian, a pillar of society, a politician or a teacher. A physical or mental handicap or growing older may impose far less in the way of specialness, sexually, than other of the aforementioned "conditions" which we take for granted.

In focusing attention upon persons with temporary or permanent handicaps, it has been the intention of this volume to help make it clear that the sex adjustment problems of such groups differ in degree but not really in kind from the adjustment problems of everyone else. Perhaps this is why so many of the parents in our clinic for children with developmental problems have reported much useful application to their other children of what they have learned about the sexuality of their "special" children. Are such things as problems associated with contraception and parenthood education categorically different matters with regard to the "normal" and "special" group members, for example the mentally retarded? Not really. As a matter of fact, we find that carefully coached mentally retarded individuals may be more reliable users of contraception than presumably bright, informed college students who usually fail to use contraception at least at first sexual intercourse with a new partner, in spite of their awareness of likely consequences of such behavior. As for parenthood, most mentally retarded persons have very good reason to avoid having children, but so do perfectly "normal" men and women. It is, perhaps, just as important to avoid parenthood for reasons of lack of interest, preparation, knowledge and concern for children as for reasons of mental incapacity to handle the complexities of the job. Indeed, kind, patient, interested retarded persons may very well do a better job of child rearing than bright, impatient, highly verbal people anxious to be doing something else and convinced that young child rearing is a demeaning drudgery.

It would seem that during this interim period in history when people in special groups are at last becoming part of the human experience, and their rights and responsibilities are being spelled out, some designation like "special" would seem to be desirable. This is in the same sense that Black Panther and Gray Panther (a power organization of older persons) organizations are necessary ways of drawing attention to the needs and rights of other minority groups. But perhaps we may reasonably look forward to a time following this painful interim, when such labels and tactics will simply be unnecessary, when it will be sufficient just to be human beings to be eligible for whatever education, counseling or special help may be appropriate. This eligibility will be without regard to whatever now leads people to be considered special. Rather, it will be with regard to recognition of the specialness of every human being and the primacy of every individual.

The foregoing speculation about the future may seem starry-eyed, idealistic and Utopian, but I believe it to be a realistic next step in human social evolution. Over the past seventeen years, I have seen several thousand children with developmental problems of considerable variety being worked with, therapeutically, by trained volunteer university students and school teachers. Sometimes a child's specialness is visible from a distance, sometimes it is not apparent at close range. In either case, the child is very soon just one of the kids present, and that's the way their clinicians see them, not as handicapped or otherwise special kids. Of course, they may need to be pointed toward or helped to get to first base—or they may need to be helped not to attack people who get in their way or not to run away if touched. They may need to function safely and enjoy themselves at play with others without benefit of arms, etc.

The point is that they are all children who have some kind of problem needing special attention. With special attention the problem may or may not disappear. Usually the children improve. But in any event, they are perceived and dealt with first as children. Of course, whatever help or support is needed is provided. The situation is the same in our programs for older adults. What is of consequence in both programs is that people enjoy doing things together and no one seems to think in terms of membership in special groups of any kind.

In brief, our programs would seem to have demonstrated the feasibility of growing away from categorizing people as anything but people, regardless of handicapping conditions. Perhaps this will be the direction of the future. The sex education and counseling aspects of both programs are certainly in harmony with this basic philosophy and approach, as the foregoing chapters may illustrate.

INDEX

HQ
56
.J59

Johnson, Warren
Russell, 1921-

Sex education and
counseling of
special groups

220605

DATE			
NOV 1 1 19 / DEC 1 5 198			
MAR 1 7 19 / DEC 8 1988			
APR 2 1 198 / APR 4 1989			
APR 2 7 1992 / JUL 2 5 '89			
OCT 4 1983 / OCT 3 0 1990			
FEB 1 9 1985 / NOV 2 7 1990			
FEB 2 6 198 / DEC 7 1990			
APR 9 198 / FEB 2 7 199			
/ MAR 1 5 1994			
DEC 1 0 1985			
DEC 9 198 / SEP 2 0 1994			
/ SEP 1 3 2005			
APR 1 9 8			

CARD REMOVED

© THE BAKER & TAYLOR CO.